DIVINE Restoration

From COUNSELOR to Counselor

CHRISTINA L. MCCRACKEN, J.D.

DIVINE Restoration

From Counselor to Counselor

Copyright © 2013 Christina L. McCracken, J.D.

Third Printing, Second Edition—November 2019 | Printed in the USA

Prepared for publication by: HIS Publishing Group—www.hispubg.com

Cover Design by Wendy K. Walters, Palm Tree Productions

ISBN: 978-0-9898598-0-6

Library of Congress Control Number: 2013947997

Emphasis added to Scripture throughout the manuscript using bold type, italics, or underlining has been made by the author.

Other reference works drawn from include:

Young, Brad H., Meet the Rabbis-Rabbinic Thought and the Teachings of Jesus, (Mass.: Hendrickson, 2007).

Zodhiates, Spiros, Hebrew-Greek Key Word Study Bible, New American Standard Bible, Tenn: AMG Publishers, 2008.

To contact the author:

COUNSELOR to Counselor
www.Counselor-to-counselor.com

$\mathcal{A}$CKNOWLEDGEMENTS

$\mathcal{T}$his writing came through the efforts of many people, known and unknown, faithful individuals who have sought to define the purposes of the LORD for restoration throughout the ages.

This book is dedicated however, to you and to those who have gone before us fighting the good fight of faith, seeking to witness of the restoration of all things. May you personally experience *Divine Restoration* and the manifestation of the LORD's Counsel in your life.

TABLE OF CONTENTS

ᎧNTRODUCTION

ave you ever wondered why you have not experienced the manifestation of the LORD's promises in your life, in the life of your family or in your nation? Have you ever wondered why it seems as if God's promises are delayed and the promised restoration found in God's Word never seems to manifest? The children of Israel had these same questions of God. They wondered why the promises of God, given through the mouth of His prophets, had seemingly been delayed and not come to pass. They also asked the question: Where is God's promised restoration?

This book is written to declare the Counsel of the LORD for achieving restoration in your life. It is also written to provide a framework for understanding barriers that have been erected and must be removed before the LORD's intended restoration can occur. Finally, this book is written to declare the Counsel of the LORD on how to remove barriers to restoration in order that you may apprehend the manifestation of the promises of God.

The Psalmist declared the blessings associated with receiving the LORD's Counsel in his life:

> O LORD, you are the portion of my inheritance and my cup, You maintain my lot.
>
> The lines have fallen to me in pleasant places, yes I have a good inheritance.
>
> I will bless the LORD who has given me counsel. My heart also instructs me in the night seasons.
>
> I have set the LORD always before me; because He is at my right hand I shall not be moved.
>
> —PSALM 16:5-8

The word "counsel" used in Psalm 16 is the Hebrew word *ya ats*, which is a verb meaning to advise and guide. The LORD's counsel or advice used and received in our lives causes a good inheritance. The LORD's Counsel in our lives causes us to be established and not be moved or shaken. The LORD's Counsel is timeless and immutable:

> The LORD brings the counsel of the nations to nothing; He makes the plans of the people of no effect.
>
> The counsel of the LORD stands forever, the plans of His heart to all generations.
>
> —PSALM 33:10-11

The word "counsel" used in Psalm 33 is the word *etsah* from the word *ya ats,* but in this context it is a noun meaning advice or plan.

Putting these two words for counsel together one would say, "The LORD's *ya ats* (advice) for you is to receive His *etsah* (plans and intents) for you." Those plans and intents are for restoration.

Restoration in every form and facet is the heart of God. From Genesis to Revelation, restoration is woven throughout Scripture because restoration is the intent of the LORD for His creation. Because restoration is the intent of the LORD, the LORD makes known His Counsel to us so that we can obtain His full and intended restoration here and now.

The Hebrew word for "restore" is *shub,* which means to turn back, return, retrieve and reverse. God's plans and intents for His creation is to restore His creation back to Him in every aspect and dimension.

The Apostle Peter declared that the Son of God, Jesus Christ the Messiah, has been received into heaven and cannot return to earth until the restoration of all things:

> "Repent, therefore and be converted, that your sins may be blotted out, so that times of refreshing may come from the presence of the Lord, and that He may send Jesus Christ, who was preached to you before, whom heaven must receive until the times of restoration of all things, which God has spoken by the mouth of all His holy prophets since the world began."
>
> —ACTS 3:19-21

Peter, having just witnessed the healing of a lame man at the gate Beautiful, proclaims to the men of Israel the only way to receive the same healing and full restoration that came to the lame beggar:

> Men of Israel, why do you marvel at this? Or why look so intently at us, as though by our own power or godliness we had made this man walk?

The God of Abraham, Isaac, and Jacob, the God of our fathers, glorified, His servant Jesus, whom you delivered up and denied in the presence of Pilate, when he was determined to let Him go.

But you denied the Holy One and the Just, and asked for a murderer to be granted to you, and killed the Prince of life, whom God raised from the dead, of which we are all witnesses.

And His name, through faith in His name, has made this man strong, whom you see and know. Yes, the faith which comes through Him has given him this perfect soundness in the presence of you all.

Yet now, brethren, I know that you did it in ignorance, as did also your rulers.

But those things which God foretold by the mouth of all His prophets, that the Christ would suffer, He has thus fulfilled.

Repent therefore and be converted, that your sins may be blotted out, so that times of refreshing may come from the presence of the Lord,

And that He may send Jesus Christ, who was preached to you before,

Whom heaven must receive until the time of restoration of all things, which God has spoken by the mouths of all His holy prophets since the world began.

—ACTS 3:12-21

In his sermon, Peter directs the men of Israel to their sin of unbelief, the sin that caused a departure from and refusal to obey the LORD. The Apostle beckons repentance so that the sin that separated them from their restoration and recovery could be blotted out.

The phrase "blotted out" is from the Greek word *exaleipho* and means to wipe out or wash. It also metaphorically signifies a removal or obliteration of something. Once sin is blotted out, restoration is possible. Until then, there can be no restoration, no refreshing and no healing.

Three keys are found in Peter's sermon that are essential for restoration and recovery. First is knowledge of the sin that has separated us from God. Second is a willingness to repent of the sin and return to God.

The word "repent" is the Greek word *metanoeo* and means to think differently, to have a change of mind. The word "return" is the Greek word *apostrophe* which means to convert, return, or to cause to return from error. Metaphorically is it spoken of a return to good. Thus, we must be willing to have a change of mind about the sin and turn from the sin toward God.

Finally, not only must there be repentance and a return to God, but we must be willing to receive the blotting out of sin, so that we can receive the refreshing that comes from the presence of the LORD. The word "refreshing" comes from the word *anapsuxis,* which means the recovery of breath, and figuratively, it means revival. When a person acknowledges his sin, turns from sin toward God and receives forgiveness for sin, then the requirements are met for refreshing to come—the recovery of the LORD's breath or revival in your life.

This book will instruct you in how to seek the LORD and ready yourself to receive the LORD's Counsel for identifying barriers and obstructions to the recovery of the Lord's breath (i.e. restoration) in your life. The process of restoration can be found in the acronym for YES: Yielded, Exposed and Surrendered.

Restoration comes when we yield our will to the will of God, honestly allow God to expose the problem, and then surrender our lives to the

Counsel of the LORD for recovery. Like the lame beggar at the gate Beautiful, we can then exclaim, "I have been made whole!" It is then that we experience *Divine Restoration*.

THE RESTORATION OF BIRTHING

"I am calling you. I am calling you. I am calling you." God's audible voice was clear and unmistakable. It was February 1994, and I had been fasting for three days, seeking the LORD for instruction on several matters. I attended an evening service at my church, and while listening to the testimony of a missionary, God spoke these words to me: "I am calling you. I am calling you. I am calling you."

When I heard the LORD's voice, I was stunned. His voice was loud and strong. The voice sounded like it came from the balcony behind me. I turned around to see if others had noticed the voice. No one appeared to have heard the sound.

The Scriptures state God spoke audibly on many occasions, often when He called a person to a task or assignment. For example,

- God spoke out loud to Moses from a burning bush and called him to lead the nation of Israel out of slavery in Egypt.[1]

- Saul of Tarsus (later to be renamed the Apostle Paul) heard the audible voice of God on the road to Damascus. God commanded Saul to follow Him and "be a witness to all men of what you have seen and heard."[2]

- God also spoke from heaven to the Apostle Peter and told him to "arise and eat" and not to call what God called clean as common.[3] God gave Peter the revelation that the same gift of salvation by grace offered to the Jew through Jesus Christ was equally available to all Gentiles. After this encounter, Peter was sent to a non-Jew, a God-fearing man, to preach the gospel to a Gentile for the first time.

- The Apostle John was in the spirit on the Lord's day when he heard God speak, a loud voice, as of a trumpet.[4] During this encounter, the Lord called John to write the things which he had seen, the things which are and the things which will take place.[5]

When the service concluded, I told an elder woman sitting next to me what had occurred. She said, "Go home and relax, I am sure God is going to speak to you tonight."

I went home and went to sleep. After several hours however, I was awakened by the awesome presence of God that filled my bedroom, a presence that caused my body to become paralyzed and motionless. I

---

1. Exodus 3
2. Acts 9:4-16, 22:14-15
3. Acts 10:13,15
4. Revelation 1:10-11
5. Revelation 1:19

was unable to move my head, hands, fingers, legs, arms, feet or toes—only my eyes could move. I looked to the left to see my clock on the side of the bed. It read 3:00 a.m. Immediately, the Spirit of God hit my chest with power. I liken the hit to a bolt of lightning that sent a power force down my body and through my feet. This happened three times, one right after the other. After the third time, I was immediately caught up in the clouds, out of my body and the LORD Jesus Christ appeared in front of me.

When I saw the LORD, He had on a white garment. I had no fear in His presence; instead, I felt intensely mesmerized about what had just happened. I immediately began talking, asking questions regarding matters on my heart. The LORD answered each question in the affirmative. After I finished speaking, He turned toward His left and He opened His arms as if to unveil something.

When the LORD opened His arms, I saw Earth below covered from side to side in two white webs, each touching the other at their ends. Then He said, "I am calling you. I am calling you. I am calling you." It was the same strong voice saying the same words I had heard in church the night before. Then, as instantaneously as I was caught up, I was back in my room. I looked at the clock next to my bed. The display read 3:45 a.m.

Over the course of the next several years, the meaning of the two webs covering Earth and the LORD's calling was defined. The vision is what was described in the Old Testament book of Isaiah, Chapter 59. In this chapter, the prophet Isaiah describes the nation of Israel and her people separated from God, overtaken by injustice, oppression and falsehood. The picture painted by the prophet was a nation and people covered in a web of lies and falsehoods.[6]

---

6.   Isaiah 59:5-6

The webs described by Isaiah had been created by religious and government leaders lying and rebelling against God and His laws. The leaders were speaking words of oppression and revolt against God, the result of which brought forth the birthing of falsehoods and lies which created webs that covered the nation and the people. The webs became a barrier between the people and God. Because of this barrier, God's justice, righteousness, truth and could not enter the fabric of the nation nor could it enter the lives of the people to bring the LORD's intended deliverance and restoration to the land and the people.

JUSTICE IS GOD'S MANDATE

Isaiah Chapter 59 describes a nation and people ensnared in lies. The prophet describes leaders who failed to plead for justice and call for truth. Yet, instead of rejecting the lies and embracing truth, the people had fallen prey to the voices of the leaders. Consequently, the people became ensnared like prey in a spider's web.[7]

Isaiah describes the iniquity of the leaders, as well as the people, as follows:

> But your iniquities have separated you from your God; and your sins have hidden His face from you, so that He will not hear.
>
> For your hands are defiled with blood, and your fingers with iniquity; your lips have spoken lies, your tongue has muttered perversity.
>
> No one calls for justice, nor does any plead for truth. They trust in empty words and speak lies; they conceive evil and bring forth iniquity.

---

7.   Isaiah 59:4

They hatch vipers' eggs and weave the spider's web; he who eats of their eggs dies, and from that which is crushed a viper breaks out.

Their webs will not become garments, nor will they cover themselves with their works; their works are works of iniquity, and the act of violence is in their hands.

Their feet run to evil, and they make haste to shed innocent blood; their thoughts are thoughts of iniquity; wasting and destruction are in their paths.

The way of peace they have not known, there is no justice in their ways; they have made themselves crooked paths; whoever takes that way shall not know peace."

—ISAIAH 59:2-8

The word for "justice" used by the prophet is the Hebrew word *mishpat* and means a legal decision by God to be followed by His people. Isaiah describes a nation that has rejected God's justice. God had given the nation righteous and holy laws, commandments, statutes and judgments to live by. The people were to heed and obey these directives so they could be used as God's instrument to establish His justice on Earth.[8] Justice in the actions of the people toward each other and the stranger was a central theme in the LORD's counsel to the nation. Exodus 23 outlines the LORD's righteous and just dealings, person to person, neighbor to neighbor:

You shall not circulate a false report. Do not put your hand with the wicked to be an unrighteous witness.

---

8.   Exodus 20:1-17

You shall not follow a crowd to do evil; nor shall you testify in a dispute so as to turn aside after many to pervert justice. You shall not show partiality to a poor man in his dispute.

If you meet your enemy's ox or his donkey going astray, you shall surely bring it back to him again. If you see the donkey of one who hates you lying under its burden, and you would refrain from helping it, you shall surely help him with it.

You shall not pervert the judgment of your poor in his dispute. Keep yourself far from a false matter; do not kill the innocent and righteous. For I will not justify the wicked. And you shall take no bribe, for a bribe blinds the discerning and perverts the words of the righteous.

Also you shall not oppress a stranger, for you know the heart of a stranger, because you were strangers in the land of Egypt.

—EXODUS 23:1-9

Executing and doing justice— person to person, neighbor to neighbor— was the mandate of God because executing justice equaled righteousness before the LORD.

The prophet Jeremiah states:

Stand in the gate of the LORD's house, and proclaim there this word, and say, "Hear the word of the LORD, all you of Judah who enter in at these gates to worship the LORD!"

Thus says the LORD of hosts, the God of Israel: "Amend your ways and your doings and I will cause you to dwell in this place. Do not trust in these lying words, saying, 'The temple of the LORD, the temple of the LORD, the temple of the LORD are these.'

"For if you thoroughly amend your ways and your doings, if you thoroughly execute judgment {mishpat} between a man and his neighbor, if you do not oppress the stranger and the fatherless, and the widow, and do not shed innocent blood in this place, or walk after other gods to your hurt, then I will cause you to dwell in this place, in the land that I gave to your fathers forever and ever."

—JEREMIAH 7:2-7

The prophet Ezekiel states:

If he has not oppressed anyone, but has restored to the debtor his pledge; has robbed not one by violence, but has given his bread to the hungry and covered the naked with clothing;

If he has not exacted usury nor taken any increase, but has withdrawn his hand from iniquity and executed true judgment {mishpat} between man and man;

If he has walked in My statutes and kept My judgments faithfully—He is just; he shall surely live!" says the Lord God.

—EZEKIEL 18:7-9

Failure of the nation to honor the mandates of God in rightly executing justice, person to person and neighbor to neighbor, was a rejection of God. As a result, the nation was covered in a web of lies, a condition that eliminated righteousness, justice, truth and equity from being found in the fabric of the nation and in the actions and intents of the people. Through the rejection of God's Counsel, the nation and the people had exchanged a covering of righteousness for a covering of lies and falsehoods. Because the nation and its people had chosen to make lies their covering rather than truth, the people became separated from

God and, therefore, unable to receive God's hand of restoration and His ear of deliverance.

The prophet explains:

> Therefore justice is far from us, nor does righteousness overtake us; We look for light, but there is darkness! For brightness, but we walk in blackness!
>
> We grope for the wall like the blind, and we grope as if we had no eyes. We stumble at noonday as at twilight; we are as dead men in desolate places.
>
> We all growl like bears, and moan sadly like doves; we look for justice, but there is none; for salvation, but it is far from us.
>
> For our transgressions are multiplied before You, and our sins testify against us; for our transgressions are with us, and as for our iniquities, we know them:
>
> In transgressing and lying against the LORD, and departing from our God, speaking oppression and revolt, conceiving and uttering from the heart words of falsehood.
>
> Justice is turned back and righteousness stands afar off; for truth is fallen in the street, and equity cannot enter.
>
> So truth fails, and he who departs from evil makes himself a prey.
>
> —ISAIAH 59:9-15

The conditions described by Isaiah are a people drawn to rebellion and deceit, oppression and revolt, although the nation had once been called faithful and full of justice:

> How the faithful city has become a harlot! It was full of justice; righteousness lodged in it, but now murderers.

Your silver has become dross, your wine mixed with water.

Your princes are rebellious and companions of thieves; everyone loves bribes, nor does the cause of the widow come before them.

—ISAIAH 1:21-23

The conditions described by Isaiah are the same conditions we are experiencing in our nation today. These are also the same conditions experienced in all nations on Earth that have rejected the LORD's mandate of justice and truth.

When I was "caught up" to meet the LORD, and He displayed the vision of Earth, the entire planet was covered in webs. For God to issue a calling to an advocate is evidence that God (the Advocate) is ready to remove the negative conditions that have separated us from receiving the Counsel of God and have kept us from His *Divine Restoration* plan.

GOD'S COUNSEL IS FOR HIS WILL TO MANIFEST ON THE EARTH

It has always been and will always be the LORD's Counsel to have His justice, righteousness, truth and equity reflected in every facet and dimension of our lives, our families and nation. It is not the Counsel of God for individuals or nations to be ensnared in or covered in a web of lies, webs that keep God's hand of restoration stayed. It is not the Counsel of God for any individual to experience deceit and robbery in personal, business and legal transactions, neither is it God's Counsel for a nation to experience violence in their land or wasting and destruction within its borders. Instead, it is God's Counsel that violence no longer be heard in the land, neither wasting nor destruction within its borders.

In fact, God desires the walls of a family, city and nation to be called "Salvation" and the gates of access to these places to be called "Praise."[9]

God loves justice and hates robbery.[10] It is never the LORD's will for truth to "fall in the streets." Rather it is the LORD's will for our works to be directed in truth, whether personal or business, legal, governmental or religious.

It is the Counsel of God for each dimension of our lives to reflect who He is: a reflection of justice, righteousness, truth and equity for all individuals—the rich and the poor alike.

When God the Son came to earth, He gave us a model prayer to pray to the Father.[11] In this prayer, the LORD prays to the Father:

"Your kingdom come, Your will be done on earth as it is in heaven."

—LUKE 11:2

The phrase "will be done" comes from the Greek word *ginomai* and means that the will or desire of someone be done or fulfilled. In this prayer, the LORD expresses the desire of His Father—that the will of the Father be done on earth as it exists in heaven. However, if webs of lies we have sown, and lies we have believed intentionally or negligently continue to remain, justice, righteousness, truth, and equity cannot enter Earth. The result: God's Counsel for restoration will be stayed.

The reality of restoration manifesting in our lives does not happen by osmosis or through contemplative thought. It comes solely through dedicated obedience to the LORD and to the instructions in righteousness

---

9. Isaiah 60:18

10. Isaiah 61:8

11. Luke 11:2-4

found in the Holy Scriptures. As individuals, we must contend earnestly for the LORD's will to be reflected in our lives and allow the zeal of the Holy Spirit to be expressed and operate in us—person to person, neighbor to neighbor. In fairness, we cannot complain about the conditions of injustice and unrighteousness in our society and government if our own lives do not reflect justice, righteousness, truth and equity.

Psalm 92:7 declares that justice and righteousness are the foundation of the LORD's throne. The foundation of justice and righteousness is what the LORD intends to manifest here and now, and the LORD intends to use you and me to accomplish this great task.

RESTORATION IS A PROCESS

Shortly after the encounter with the LORD, I became intensely frustrated I had not personally witnessed restoration, although I believed and followed the Word of God. I began a 40-day fast seeking understanding as to why it appeared God's hand was shortened and His ear heavy that it could not hear His promises found in His Word.

During the fast, the LORD revealed layers of webs weaved over my life through lies I had believed and lies sown by others— by those in authority and by individuals I had known throughout my life. It was at that time the LORD's calling became clear. I began to understand what Isaiah meant when he described a nation and people "covered in a web of lies." Once I was able to experience this condition, I knew the LORD was ready to reveal His Counsel regarding:

1. how webs of lies are formed and

2. how to remove them so that recovery—going from loss to restoration—could become a reality.

When the 40-day fast was complete, the process of restoration began.

This book is written to bring understanding regarding how webs of falsehood are formed and how their presence keeps the LORD's Counsel and His covenant promises of restoration from entering your life. This book will also explain how to be relieved from webs of falsehoods and lies. As you read through the pages, ask the Holy Spirit to give you wisdom and revelation in the knowledge of these issues in your life. Ask the LORD to impart understanding so you gain revelation of any lies believed and any lies spoken or sown over you which have kept out the manifestation of the LORD's will in your life, your business, your family and you nation.

The LORD's name is Wonderful, Counselor, Mighty God, Everlasting Father and Prince of Peace.[12] He alone is the infallible source of all wisdom and truth and is a true and righteous Counselor.[13] He is the One who is pleading your case right now in heaven's Courts. As your Counselor and Advocate, Jesus Christ is ever living to make intercession for you at the throne of God.[14]

According to the Scriptures, the Son of God has already won your case and has secured for you a verdict of not guilty and a judgment from the Most High God's Court for a full restoration.[15] This verdict is given to every child of God, by grace through faith in Jesus Christ. This debt-free verdict and grace—filled judgment issued from the Court of God is our inheritance.[16] However, although our inheritance is freely given and has already been obtained, the manifestation of that inheritance— experiencing that inheritance in our lives—requires obedience to the LORD and His Word.

---

12. Isaiah 9:6

13. Colossians 2:2-3

14. Hebrews 7:25

15. 2 Corinthians 5:12-21, Ephesians 2:14-18, John 8:36, Galatians 5:1

16. Galatians 3:26-29, 4:1-7

THE WEBS MUST BE REMOVED

In order to receive our inheritance, webs of lies we have believed, lies we have sown, and lies that have been sown by others over our lives have to be removed. Lies and falsehoods are formed, knowingly or unknowingly, through rebellion to God as well as listening to and believing others who are in rebellion to God.

Rebellion to God is likened to the sin of witchcraft.[17] Rebellion is the force that sets in motion the weaving of webs and creates irregularities and distortions to the Counsel of God for your life. Individuals who have rebellion in their hearts are knowingly or unknowingly operating in witchcraft. Those in agreement with those in rebellion are, knowingly or unknowingly, also operating in witchcraft. Both are caught in a tangled web of lies, a barrier to God's hand of restoration and ear of deliverance.

The prophet Amos declared,

Can two walk together, unless they are agreed?

—AMOS 3:3

From this Scripture we learn that a person cannot sincerely expect God's hand of restoration and His ear of deliverance and live in rebellion to God or be in association with individuals in rebellion to God. This person is a double-minded man, a person who attempts to hold onto God with one hand and onto the world with the other. God says that if you want to make the world your friend—you want to seek

---

17.   1 Samuel 15:23

the counsel of the world, rather than the Counsel of God, you become an enemy of God.[18]

Therefore, for lies and falsehoods to be exposed and removed, our Wonderful Counselor needs our full consent and full cooperation in partnering with Him, as a client partners with his lawyer. In other words, our will must diligently obey and choose to be conformed to the will of the Counselor. If we diligently heed the Counselor and diligently follow His instructions, then garnering restoration is certain. However, if we will not heed and obey the Counselor's instructions, webs of deception and lies will remain, and we will not be recipients of the LORD's intended restoration.

Wash yourselves, make yourselves clean; put away the evil of your doings from before My eyes.

Cease to do evil, learn to do good;

Seek justice; rebuke the oppressor; defend the fatherless, plead for the widow.

"Come now, and let us reason together," says the LORD, "Though your sins are like scarlet, they shall be as white as snow; though they are red like crimson, they shall be as wool.

If you are willing and obedient, you shall eat the good of the land;

But if you refuse and rebel, you shall be devoured by the sword;" For the mouth of the LORD has spoken.

—ISAIAH 1:16-20

---

18. James 4:1-8

Thus says the LORD, your redeemer, the Holy One of Israel: "I am the LORD your God, who teaches you to profit, who leads you by the way you should go.

—ISAIAH 48:17

God promises us peace like a river and righteousness like the waves of the sea if we will heed His commandments and receive His teaching, instruction and Counsel. As you read this book, meditate on the Counsel of the LORD. Consider current or former rebellion in your life. Consider lies you have believed and lies you have sown through the agreement with others in rebellion. Consider those you have associated with throughout your life in personal and business relationships. Ask the LORD to reveal any seeds of iniquity and falsehood sown by you or over you through your association in current or former relationships, so any cords of iniquity can be broken and removed.

Meditate on the Word of God and let His Counsel go deep into your heart for personal revelation and transformation. The Counsel of God is for you to know the truth so that the truth will set you free.[19]

Remember God is pleading for you 24/7, and in doing so, He is pleading that your faith will never fail as you seek His restoration in every aspect of your life. In your pursuit, remember that God's ways are not our ways. His thoughts are much higher than our thoughts, and His ways are higher than our ways.[20] Understand that, at times, the LORD's Counsel may not make sense. During those times, surrender to the LORD your present lack of understanding and ask Him to help you understand His ways. Rest assured the LORD will always lead you

---

19. John 8:32
20. Isaiah 55:8-9

in His wisdom and by and through His peaceable fruit of righteousness that is sown in peace.

The prophet Isaiah said, "If you are willing and obedient, you will eat the good of the land; but if you refuse and rebel, you will be devoured by the sword."[21] Choose today to make it your diligent aim to be willing and obedient for therein lies your *Divine Restoration*.

---

21. Isaiah 1:19-20

THE LORD'S COUNSEL FOR YOU IS RESTORATION

There can be no dispute—the LORD's Counsel for you, your family and your nation is restoration. The Scripture proclaims that God sent His Word to heal us and to deliver us from our destructions.[22] The Word of God has the power and ability to bring restoration because the Word of God is both living and full of power.

The Scripture declares,

> The Word of God is living and powerful, sharper than any two-edged sword, piercing even to the division of the soul and spirit and of joints and marrow, and is a discerner of the thoughts and intents of the heart.
>
> —HEBREWS 4:12

---

22. Psalm 107:20

The word "living" in Hebrews 4:12 is the Greek word *dzah* which is a verb meaning to live or living, the opposite of what is dead, inactive or transient. The word "power" in Hebrews 4:12 is the Greek word *energes* and means something at work, full of energy, active and effective. The Word of God is alive and full of active and effective power—power to heal, power to transform and power to restore because Jesus Christ is the Word of God, the living *logos* (written, declared or spoken communication or divine utterance). The Scripture says,

> In the beginning was the Word, and the Word was with God and the Word was God.
>
> —JOHN 1:1

> and the Word became flesh and dwelt among us, and we beheld His glory, the glory as of the only begotten of the Father, full of grace and truth …
>
> —JOHN 1:14

> For the law was given through Moses, but grace and truth came through Jesus Christ. No one has seen God at any time. The only begotten Son, who is in the bosom of the Father, He has declared Him.
>
> —JOHN 1:17-18

God the Father manifested Himself to His creation through the person of His Son, Jesus Christ, the Messiah. In the beginning existed the Word and the Word was God, and the Word put on flesh and lived among us in the person of Jesus Christ who is the living Word of God.

When the Apostle Peter proclaimed to the lame beggar at the gate Beautiful, "Silver and gold I do not have, but what I do have I give you.

In the name of Jesus Christ of Nazareth, rise and walk,"[23] Peter was declaring that in and through this Name and this Name only, healing and perfect restoration comes.

Restoration is found only in and through the Name of Jesus Christ of Nazareth. When Jesus Christ declared, "It is finished," and took His last breath on a Roman cross, His death declared before heaven, Earth and all things under Earth that He had paid every debt owed to the Father that was necessary to restore creation back into fellowship and union with the Father.[24] God sending His Son to die for the world is infallible proof of the Father's unwavering desire to restore His creation.

It is important to accept this simple but highly profound truth. If not, you will have a difficult time receiving restoration and will be prone to look to other substitutes or world-related remedies.

Many Christians have been attending church for years, and sincerely love and seek to obey the LORD, but have never obtained restoration in their lives. Most Christian's I have met live with feelings of personal condemnation, guilt and shame, never experiencing the freedom that Jesus Christ gave them through His atoning death on the cross. Many Christian's have not rightly discerned their personal and business relationships and have formed alliances with individuals who have rebellion in their heart and speak words of falsehoods out of their mouths. These individuals wonder why they do not experience the manifestation of God's promised restoration and live in a less-than restored state.

Other Christian's have separated from ungodly alliances, but don't realize that unrighteous agreements made while in these former relationships are still active and alive in the unseen realm of the Spirit.

---

23. Acts 3:6

24. John 19:30

Until these unrighteous agreements are nullified or cancelled, these agreements form a barrier to restoration.

By analogy, a divorce or personal or business dissolution is a good example. Many individuals believe that the relationship with the other spouse or business partner ends at the time the Decree of Divorce is signed by the Court or the business or personal relationship is dissolved. All who have experienced a divorce or personal or business dissolution know there is a period where clean-up after the divorce or dissolution occurs. This is a time where emotional and/or financial matters are addressed, and recovery is sought. The divorce or dissolution only initiates a physical severance of the relationship. Whereas, the restoration process requires addressing any "webs" that may have been created during the former relationship that would now keep you from the LORD's full restoration.

I recall teaching at a Women's gathering with several hundred women. At the noon hour, we had corporate and individual prayer. One of the last women that I prayed for had been diagnosed with fibromyalgia, a condition that causes musculoskeletal pain. She had not walked without a cane for 2 years. After I asked her a series of questions, the LORD showed me that the condition she was experiencing had been created by her former husband speaking curses over her life. These word curses (lies) released from the mouth of her husband, who at the time was her spiritual covering, created "webs" over her life. These "webs of lies" had now become her covering. Once we renounced the word curses and she forgave her former husband, the anointing of the LORD came and immediately healed her body. She said she felt heat go through her body and she knew she was healed. She threw away her cane and stared running around the church celebrating.

The prophet Nahum declares, "God is good.[25]" The word "good" is the Hebrew word *tob* meaning, good, pleasant, whatever is right,

---

25. Nahum 1:7

and happy. Because God's very nature and character is good and pleasant, God's thoughts and intents toward you are only good and pleasant, no matter what circumstances you have experienced or what circumstances you are currently experiencing. The bottom line: God's thoughts toward you are good and pleasant, and He desperately desires you to experience the reality of those thoughts in your life.

> Many, O LORD my God, are Your wonderful works which You have done; and your thoughts toward us cannot be recounted to You in order; If I would declare and speak of them, they are more than can be numbered.
>
> —PSALM 40:5

For a moment, consider the profound concept that God's good thoughts toward you are more than can be numbered. I tried to wrap my mind around this eternal truth and asked myself, "Who do I know that has had only good thoughts toward me?" In fact, who in this world has only good thoughts toward another? The answer is simple, no one. No human can fit that extraordinary bill, but the concept of so many good thoughts coming from the mind of God intrigued me.

One day while praying, the LORD opened the spirit realm and in a split second displayed before and around me His innumerable good thoughts toward me. In that moment, I was surrounded by the more-than-can-be-numbered thoughts of God. All that flooded my understanding were the pleasant and good thoughts of God toward me. The entire atmosphere was filled with God's glory, His goodness toward me, the expression of His very nature.

GOD'S THOUGHTS TOWARD YOU
ARE FOR RESTORATION

As we come into the mindset that God is good and only has pleasant thoughts toward us, we activate the process of allowing the Word of God to conform our mind to the mind of God. When this process happens, we begin to accept as fact and believe by faith that God intends our restoration.

The Scripture declares that as a man thinks in his heart, so is he.[26] In order for restoration to occur, we need the LORD to change our "heart thinking."

Listen to the heart of God:

> For I know the thoughts that I think toward you, says the LORD, thoughts of peace and not of evil, to give you a future and a hope.
>
> —JEREMIAH 29:11

This Scripture is a perfect description of God's thoughts and intents towards His creation. The Hebrew word for "thoughts" is the word *machashabah,* which means the plans of God. The Hebrew word for "peace" is the word *shalom* and means completeness, wholeness, peace, health, welfare, safety, soundness, tranquility, prosperity, perfectness, fullness, rest, and harmony. The Hebrew word for "evil" is the word *rah,* which means adversity, affliction, calamity, grief, misery, sorrow and trouble. The Hebrew word for "future" is the word *achariyth,* which means length, posterity, residue or reward. The Hebrew word for "hope" is the word *tiqvah* and means expectation, something yearned for and anticipated

---

26. Proverbs 23:7

eagerly. Placing the meaning of these words into the Scripture causes us to experience a deeper reflection of God's thoughts and intents toward us:

> For I know the plans and thoughts that I think toward you, says the LORD, thoughts of completeness, wholeness, peace, health, welfare, safety, soundness, tranquility, prosperity, perfectness, fullness, rest and harmony, and not of adversity, affliction, calamity, grief, misery, sorrow or trouble, in order to give you length of posterity and reward as well as an expectation anticipated for eagerly.

The prophet Jeremiah was given these words to write in a letter to Jewish exiles who had been taken as prisoners and held as captive slaves in Babylon. The exiles had been removed from their home in Canaan, leaving behind their beloved temple in Jerusalem, the center of their religious life. In 586 B.C., the temple was burned by the Babylonian army as prophesied by both Jeremiah and Isaiah. During the Babylonian siege, many of the religious and civic leaders had been killed, and Judah's last king, Zedekiah, was deported, his sons killed, and his eyes put out.[27] The death and exile of many of Judah's leaders, along with the destruction of the temple, instantly removed the fabric that had previously held the southern kingdom of Israel and its society together.

The promise of restoration through the prophet to the Jewish exiles living in a foreign land with no temple, no king, and no kingdom was profound. The thought of a future hope and fulfillment of the covenant promise of restoration was illusory to some and almost more than could be believed by others. Whether or not these promises were believed, God had given the promises and He was going to fulfill them to a believing and faithful remnant.

---

27. 2 Kings 25:1-7

The LORD declared to the exiles that after the nation had served a seventy-year sentence for their rebellion against Him, He would return to the remnant and perform His good Word to them (Jeremiah 29:10). God declared He was going to return the remnant to their home, and He was going to restore their land and their temple, the place of worship. Once the place of worship was restored, God would return to the nation with the glory of His divine presence.

Through both Isaiah and Jeremiah, God reassured the exiles that although they had experienced punishment, exile, and great disaster, Yahweh (the covenant name for God) would faithfully perform the terms of His covenant to them. He declares:

> Thus says the LORD, your Redeemer, and He who formed you from the womb: "I am the LORD, who makes all things, who stretches out the heavens all alone, who spreads abroad the earth by Myself;
>
> "Who frustrates the signs of the babblers, and drives diviners mad; who turns wise men backward, and makes their knowledge foolishness;
>
> "Who confirms the word of His servant, and performs the counsel of His messengers; who says to Jerusalem, 'You shall be inhabited.' To the cities of Judah, 'You shall be built,' and I will raise up her waste places."
>
> —ISAIAH 44:24-26

God was expectantly awaiting the end of the nation's divine sentence of judgment in order to restore the nation, return the exiles to their covenant land, rebuild the city of Jerusalem and the house of worship and restore the cities of Judah. Just as the LORD was expectantly waiting to perform His good Word to the nation of Israel, He is expectantly and eagerly waiting to perform His good Word toward you.

You will find throughout this book living, crimson veins and arteries that flow from the heart of God. You will hear the heartbeat of God toward you—His Counsel of peace and not calamity. Is it possible to have restoration and recovery after profound devastation? The answer is a resounding YES!

Isaiah clearly outlines the LORD's intent and heart concerning restoration after captivity:

> For in My wrath I struck you, but in My favor I have had mercy on you.
>
> Therefore your gates shall be open continually; they shall not be shut day or night, that men may bring to you the wealth of the Gentiles, and their kings in procession.
>
> For the nation and kingdom which will not serve you shall perish, and those nations shall be utterly ruined.
>
> The glory of Lebanon shall come to you, the cypress, the pine and the box tree together, to beautify the place of My sanctuary; and I will make the place of My feet glorious.
>
> Also the sons of those who afflicted you shall come bowing to you, and all those who despised you shall fall prostrate at the soles of your feet; and they shall call you The City of The LORD, Zion the Holy One of Israel.
>
> Whereas you have been forsaken and hated, so that no one went through you, I will make you an eternal excellence, a joy of many generations.

You shall milk the breast of kings; you shall know that I, the LORD, am your Savior and your Redeemer, the Mighty One of Jacob.

Instead of bronze I will bring gold, instead of iron I will bring silver, instead of wood bronze, instead of stones, iron. I will make your officers peace, and your magistrates' righteousness.

Violence shall no longer be heard in your land, neither wasting, nor destruction within your borders; but you shall call your walls Salvation and your gates Praise.

—ISAIAH 60:10-18

The attributes of Divine Restoration are gloriously summarized by the LORD through Isaiah in these verses: mercy, wealth, glory, beauty, eternal excellence, the joy of many generations, peace and praise. The description of restoration in Isaiah 60:10-18 is nothing short of describing God's very gracious and good nature. In Isaiah Chapter 61, we are told how restoration will be accomplished:

The Spirit of the Lord GOD is upon me, because the Lord has anointed me to preach good tidings to the poor, He has sent me to heal the broken hearted, to proclaim liberty to the captives, and the opening of the prison to those who are bound;

To proclaim the acceptable year of the LORD, and the day of vengeance of our God; to comfort all who mourn,

To console those who mourn in Zion, to give them beauty for ashes, the oil of joy for mourning, the garment of praise for the spirit of heaviness; that they may be called trees of righteousness, the planting of the LORD, that He may be glorified.

And they shall rebuild the old ruins, they shall raise up the former desolations, and they shall repair the ruined cities, the desolations of many generations.

—ISAIAH 61:1-4

It is through the Spirit of the Lord that restoration is accomplished. Isaiah 61:1-2 is the first passage in the Hebrew Bible that Jesus Christ proclaimed in the temple at the beginning of His earthly ministry.[28] After Jesus read this passage, He closed the Scriptures, gave it to another, sat down and declared, "Today, this Scripture is fulfilled in your hearing." All present in the temple bore witness to Him and marveled at the gracious words that proceeded out of His mouth.[29] The word for "gracious" used is the Greek word *charis,* which means favor, gift, liberality, pleasure, and elegance. Can you hear the Lord declaring, "Look to Me for I AM He who fulfills this Scripture, I AM He who brings your restoration, I AM He from whom the very essence of grace, favor, pleasure, and elegance flows, I AM your healing, I AM your liberty, and I AM your deliverer?"

Through Jesus Christ we each can receive full restoration as pronounced in Isaiah 60:10-18. Even if you have *heard* the gospel of the Kingdom before, it is time for you to *experience* the fullness of it.

Romans 1:16 declares that the gospel is the power of God unto salvation to everyone who believes, to the Jew first and to the Greek. The word "salvation" in Romans 1:16 is the Greek word *soteria,* a word that means deliverance, soundness, prosperity, happiness, rescue, well-being. Jesus Christ declared deliverance, soundness, prosperity,

---

28. Luke 4:16-22

29. Luke 4:22

happiness, rescue and well-being. The gospel of the Kingdom of God is the good news of the Father, proclaimed through the Son.

RESTORATION REVEALED THROUGH THE SON

When the Son of God came to earth, He had only one mission: to give His life as a ransom for many.[30] The word "ransom" is the Greek word *lutron* and means "to loose" or to release from slavery or captivity brought about by the payment of a price, and includes a price paid for the penalty of a debt. The blood of Jesus Christ was the purchase price for our reconciliation back to the Father. Restoration, divinely purchased by the blood of Jesus Christ, includes:

1. **deliverance** from the power (*exousia*, authority or right to act) of darkness,

2. **conveyance** into the Kingdom of God,

3. **redemption** (*apolutrosis*m payment of a ransom, deliverance or setting free), and

4. **forgiveness** (*aphesis*, "to send away," dismissal cancellation of debt or punishment) of sins.[31]

The embodiment of the gospel message is restoration of peace between God and man. Peace between God and man is what God intends to bring into your life, the life of your family and your nation.

Although salvation is freely given to all, like any gift it must be received. However, simply receiving God's Counsel will not automatically bring its manifestation in your life. In order to obtain the manifestation of

30. Matthew 20:28

31. Colossians 1:12-14

God's Counsel in our lives, we must be willing to diligently *listen and obey* the Counsel of the LORD.

The prophet Isaiah says,

> Ho! Everyone who thirsts, come to the waters; and you who have no money, come buy and eat. Yes, come, buy wine and milk without money and without price.
>
> Why do you spend money for what is not bread, and your wages for what does not satisfy? Listen carefully to Me, and eat what is good, and let your soul delight itself in abundance.
>
> Incline your ear, and come to me. Hear, and your soul shall live; and I will make an everlasting covenant with you—the sure mercies of David.
>
> —ISAIAH 55:1-3

In this prophesy, God issues a summons for the Jews in exile to remove all Babylonian influences in their lives and come to Him that they may freely enjoy His abundance of grace, a meal that will eternally satisfy. In order to obtain this free abundance, worldly detachments and influences must be removed. The people must choose to listen carefully to and hear the voice of the LORD, rather than worldly voices and influences. The Hebrew word used in this passage both for "listen carefully" and "hear" is the word *shema*. The word *shema* means not only to hear but also to act and obey. It is the same word used in Deuteronomy 6:4, when the LORD says,

Hear, O, Israel: The LORD our God, the LORD is one!

When we fail to listen to God and obey His Word of truth, we reject our only hope for restoration. As a result, we end up listening to and obeying something other than truth. That something comes to us in the form of lies—lies about God, lies about ourselves, lies about others, and lies about our own condition as we stand before a Holy God. Before we know it, we are no longer accepting truth as our foundation. Instead, we are accepting and believing lies as our foundation and wearing lies as our covering. This is the condition that existed in the land of Israel and the reason God was not hearing the nation's prayer for restoration and deliverance.[32]

Isaiah 59 describes a people who had departed from God by listening to religious and government leaders who were speaking oppression and revolt by conceiving and uttering from the heart words of falsehood.[33] Because the people chose to agree with and listen to falsehoods, they rebelled against God and despised His Counsel. As a result, sin increased, iniquity abounded and the people began to conceive evil from their hearts, birthing webs of iniquity. The iniquity became like a spider's web covering the individuals of the nation.[34]

Consequently, a barrier was erected between the people and God so that justice was turned back, righteousness stood afar off, truth fell in the street, and equity could not enter into the lives of the people or the nation.[35] This condition caused the hand of El Gabor, the Mighty God, metaphorically to be "shortened" and God's ear that always heard the cry of His people, metaphorically to be "heavy" so that it could not hear.[36]

The Apostle James tells us that when we make the world our friend, when we draw close to the world and its influences, we become an enemy of God and are likened to an adulterous wife:

---

32. Isaiah 59
33. Isaiah 59:13
34. Isaiah 59:1-6
35. Isaiah 59:14-15
36. Isaiah 59:1

Adulterers and adulteresses! Do you not know that friendship with the world is enmity with God? Whoever therefore wants to be a friend of the world makes himself an enemy of God.

Or do you think that the Scripture says in vain, "The Spirit who dwells in us yearns jealously?"

But He gives more grace. Therefore He says: "God resists the proud, but gives grace to the humble."

Therefore, submit to God. Resist the devil and he will flee from you.

Draw near to God and He will draw near to you. Cleanse your hands, you sinners; and purify your hearts, you double-minded.

Lament and mourn and weep! Let your laughter be turned to mourning and your joy to gloom.

Humble yourselves in the sight of the Lord, and He will lift you up.

—JAMES 4:4-10

Drawing near to God is always the solution. The Greek word for "draw near" used by the Apostle is the word *eggizo*, which means to approach, come near to and worship God with a pious heart. The more you draw near to God and show Him that you are sincerely choosing Him over the influences of the world, the more you are able to break free of the lies that have hindered His voice and Counsel from entering your life.

As you sincerely draw near to God and ask Him to cleanse your heart from the influences of the world, your heart will be able to hear the voice of truth and not the father of lies. In hearing and heeding the voice of truth, you will have vision to remove the web of lies that have hindered restoration and withheld the hand of deliverance.

The following chapter outlines the importance of seeking the Counsel of God for restoration. Chapters thereafter identify barriers to restoration and explain how those barriers can be removed. The final chapters are intended to stir up faith, a driving faith, that allows no room for retreat or compromise until you have experienced *Divine Restoration*.

SEEKING THE COUNSEL OF GOD

ne of the clearest and best accounts of restoration obtained through seeking the Counsel of God is found in 1 Samuel 30. By way of background, this is the story of David, a shepherd boy, chosen by God to be king of Israel. Although David had previously been anointed by the prophet Samuel to be king, he had not yet taken the throne. Rather, we find David fleeing for his life, running from Saul, the reigning king of Israel. King Saul was resentful and jealous of David because God had given this shepherd boy many victories against Israel's enemies. A picture of how King Saul's jealousy of David developed is found in 1 Samuel 18:6-9:

> Now it happened as they were coming home, when David was returning from the slaughter of the Philistines, that the women had come out of all the cities of Israel, singing and dancing, to meet King Saul, with tambourines, with joy, and with musical instruments. So the women sang as they danced, and said: "Saul

has slain his thousands, and David his ten thousands." Then Saul was very angry, and the saying displeased him; and he said, "They have ascribed to David ten thousands, and to me they have ascribed only thousands. Now what more can he have but the kingdom?" So Saul eyed David from that day forward.

It is important to note that David did nothing to cause an "evil eye" from King Saul. Scripture tells us that David was blameless before the Lord concerning King Saul.[37]

Nevertheless, King Saul sought to kill David. As a result, David ran for his life and ended up in the camp of the Philistines, the dreaded enemies of Israel. 1 Samuel 29 provides the account of the Philistine rulers controversy with David when he sought to align himself with the Philistines as an ally against King Saul and, therefore, against the children of Israel. As you can imagine, it would not be the Counsel of the LORD for the anointed and future king of Israel to be sent out to battle *against* the armies of Israel.

As God would have it, the Philistines ultimately rejected David's desire to go to battle alongside of them, fearing he would turn on them to regain favor with King Saul.[38] Consequently, David and his men returned to their camp in Ziklag, a Philistine city. However, when they arrived, David and his men found the entire camp burned with fire and all the women and children taken captive as a result of an overnight invasion by the Amalekites.[39]

The Amalekites were fierce enemies of Israel. They were descendants of Esau, the father of the Edomites. King Agag, king of the Amalekites,

---

37. 1 Samuel 19:4, 1 Samuel 24:6-22

38. 1 Samuel 29:4-11

39. 1 Samuel 30:1-3

was supposed to have been killed by King Saul years prior as punishment for Amalek attacking the rear ranks of Israel when they were coming out of Egypt.[40] At the time of that attack, the LORD issued a decree concerning the conduct of Amalek toward the nation of Israel and said,

> Therefore it shall be, when the LORD your God has given you rest from your enemies all around, in the land which the LORD your God is giving you to possess as an inheritance, that you will blot out the remembrance of Amalek from under heaven. You shall not forget.
>
> —DEUTERONOMY 25:19

God does not forget His righteous judgments. Because kings were appointed by God to execute His judgments on Earth, God had instructed King Saul to attack Amalek and utterly destroy all they had and "spare them not."[41] However, King Saul did not heed the of the LORD to destroy all the Amalekites. As a result of King Saul's defiance toward God's counsel, God sent the prophet Samuel to him to declare his removal as king:

> Has the LORD as great delight in burnt offerings and sacrifices, as in obeying the voice of the LORD? Behold, to obey is better than sacrifice, and to heed than the fat of rams. For rebellion is as the sin of witchcraft, and stubbornness is as iniquity and idolatry. Because you have rejected the word of the LORD, He also has rejected you from being king.
>
> —1 SAMUEL 15:22-23

---

40. 1 Samuel 15:2, Deuteronomy 25:17-19

41. 1 Samuel 15:3

Following this incident, God instructed Samuel to anoint David as the new king of Israel.[42] Once David was anointed as Israel's king, the anointing of kingship left Saul. Scripture declares that the Spirit of the LORD departed from Saul, and a distressing spirit from the LORD troubled him.[43] Although the anointing of the LORD's Spirit had left Saul, transference of kingdom rule and kingdom reign to David had not yet taken place. Although God had rejected Saul as king, Saul was not ready to surrender and relinquish his position as king. Rather, he became jealous of David, and his jealousy turned into a desire to murder David. As a result, David fled from King Saul, ultimately hiding in the camp of the Philistines.

At this time in David's life, David needed divine help, divine restoration and divine vindication. David was innocent of the accusation of treason lodged against him by King Saul, and although he had been chosen and anointed as king of Israel, he did not yet have a throne. Rather, he was running to save his life, hiding in the camp of the enemies of Israel.

1 Samuel 30 declares the account of the Ziklag ambush and the beginning of David's restoration. When David and his men saw that Ziklag had been burned and all their families and possessions taken, David and his men "lifted up their voices and wept, until they had no more power to weep."[44] However, what happens next is a golden key that opens the door to restoration. The Scripture declares that David "strengthened himself in the LORD his God."[45] The Hebrew word for "strengthened" is the word *chazaq,* which means to encourage or make

---

42. 1 Samuel 16:1-13

43. 1 Samuel 16:14

44. 1 Samuel 30:4

45. 1 Samuel 30:6

yourself strong in the LORD. To strengthen himself in the LORD, David went to Abiathar the priest and said,

> Please bring the ephod here to me. Abiathar brought the ephod to David. So David inquired of the LORD saying, "Shall I pursue this troop? Shall I overtake them?" And the LORD answered him, "Pursue, for you shall surely overtake them and without fail recover all."
>
> —1 SAMUEL 30:8

In this account, we learn several keys for obtaining restoration. First, David inquired of the LORD. Next, David waited to hear from the LORD to find out 1) if God wanted David to attack Ziklag, 2) if God wanted David to recover what had been taken and 3) how David was to go about finding, attacking and recovering his family and possessions. Immediately after David inquired of the LORD, the LORD provided him with direction, guidance and aid for his recovery. Promising that David would recover all, the LORD instructs David to go forward and pursue the Amalekites, "Pursue, for you shall surely overtake them and without fail recover all."[46]

The LORD not only tells David he is going to recover all he lost, but also supplies the necessary provision for David to do it. The Scripture states that an Egyptian, a servant of one of the Amalekite masters, fell behind after the Amalekite raid.[47] This young Egyptian servant, left in the field to die, directed David and his men to where the Amalekites were camped.[48] Once David found the camp, he attacked the Amalekites from twilight until evening. The Scripture states, "Not

---

46. 1 Samuel 30:8
47. 1 Samuel 30:11-13
48. 1 Samuel 30:15-16

a man escaped" for "David recovered all that the Amalekites had carried away and nothing of theirs was lacking either small or great, sons or daughters, spoil or anything which they had taken from them, for David recovered all."[49]

When I read this account years ago it became a quick favorite. The words *recovered all, recovered all, recovered all* rang in my heart and mind. The LORD told David he was not going to fail, he would have total success, and he would recover everything—all that had been taken. David recovered all!

When a child of God recovers all, God recovers all. When a child of God is vindicated, God's great Name is vindicated. David's victory and vindication are God's victory and vindication.

Look closely. God providently set in place all circumstances and necessary provision for David to have victory during an all-out evil campaign lodged against him by King Saul. King Saul's evil desire to kill David providentially put David to flight, a flight that landed him in the camp of the Philistines. It was there that David was required to look only to God for deliverance and victory. It was the Philistine battle with Israel that caused David and his men to leave their camp in Ziklag to go to another city to war with the Philistines. It was the rejection of David by the Philistines that caused David and his men to return to Ziklag after the camp had been set on fire and their wives and children taken captive. Through God providentially allowing the Amalekites the opportunity to raid the camp of David and burn the city of Ziklag, David was given the opportunity to do what God had previously commanded King Saul to do—blot out the remembrance of the name of the Amalekites from the earth.[50]

---

49. 1 Samuel 30:17-19

50. Deuteronomy 25:19

It was also during this battle fought between the Philistines and Israel, the battle in which David was rejected from being allowed to fight in, that God allowed the death of King Saul.[51] In allowing the death of King Saul, God caused his loyal servant David to obtain the manifestation of the Counsel of God in his life and succeed to the throne as king of Israel. The Counsel of God manifesting in David's life did not occur through rebellion, deception or falsehood. Rather, the manifestation of God's Counsel came solely through David seeking and heeding the Counsel of the LORD.

SEEKING GOD'S COUNSEL ALWAYS BRINGS SUCCESS

The Scripture declares that righteousness and justice are the foundation of God's throne.[52] Every circumstance meant by King Saul to cause David's demise, God providentially used to lay the foundation for the throne of David, a throne of righteousness and justice. Once God's righteous foundation was laid for David's kingship, God ushered in His chosen king to rule on Israel's throne. David's recovery was God's recovery.

In this decisive battle, not only did God allow David to recover his wives and possessions with "not one of them missing," but also God used David to fulfill God's divine retribution on the Amalekite nation. After God's name was vindicated before the nation of Israel through David executing divine retribution on the Amalekites, David's name was vindicated before the nation of Israel. David's recovery became God's recovery. God's vindication became David's vindication.

---

51. 1 Samuel 31:4-6

52. Psalm 97:2

After King Saul died, David was anointed again, this time as king of Judah. David initially lived and ruled from Hebron for seven years and six months.[53] After this time, the tribes of Israel came to David and made a covenant with him and anointed him king over Israel.[54] After David had the allegiance of both Israel and Judah, he was ready to take the stronghold, the city of Jerusalem..

Jerusalem had been in the hands of the Jebusites since the time of Joshua, and the children of Judah had been unable to drive them out.[55] But now God was ready to grant David victory over the Jebusites. The Scripture states, "David took the stronghold of Zion," and David dwelt in the stronghold and "became great and the LORD God of Hosts was with him."[56] The Scripture also states the Philistines came down to the stronghold and deployed themselves against Israel.[57] Once again, David inquired of the LORD.

The Scripture states,

> So David inquired of the LORD, saying, "Shall I go up against the Philistines? Will You deliver them into my hand?" And the LORD said to David, "Go up, for I will doubtless deliver the Philistines into your hand."
>
> —1 CHRONICLES 14:10

---

53. 2 Samuel 5:5
54. 2 Samuel 5:1-3
55. Joshua 15:63
56. 2 Samuel 5:7-10
57. 2 Samuel 5:17-18

God delivered the Philistines into David's hand at Baal Perazim.[58] However, the Philistines left their graven images in battle, and went up once again and deployed themselves in the Valley of Rephaim.[59] Again, David inquired of LORD and the LORD responded to David with specific and direct instructions for garnering a total victory:

> "You shall not go up; circle around behind them, and come upon them in front of the mulberry trees. And it shall be, when you hear the sound of marching in the tops of the mulberry trees, then you shall advance quickly for then the LORD will go out before you to strike the camp of the Philistines." And David did so, as the LORD commanded him and he drove back the Philistines from Geba as far as Gezer.
>
> —2 SAMUEL 5:23-25

Israel's defeat of the Philistines occurred after the tribes were united and once King David dwelt in Jerusalem. But that is not all, the LORD desired to restore the Ark of God, to Jerusalem. 2 Samuel 6 is the account of King David's recovery of the Ark. Initially, King David failed to inquire of the LORD as to how to transport the Ark. This failure resulted in the death of Uzzah.[60] However, the Ark was ultimately brought by King David into the City of David after David heeded the Counsel of the LORD.[61]

The circumstances that brought King David's recovery also brought about the nation of Israel's recovery. Recovery came to King David through 1) the divine providence of God, 2) David remaining blameless

---

58. 2 Samuel 5:20

59. 2 Samuel 5:22

60. 2 Samuel 6:7

61. 2 Samuel 6:12-17

and innocent during his years of trial and testing, 3) David keeping a loyal heart of devotion to God and 4) David seeking and heeding the Counsel of the LORD.

A song of David declaring the vindication of the LORD in his life is found in Psalm 17:1-7 and states,

> Hear a just cause, O LORD, Attend to my cry; Give ear to my prayer which is not from deceitful lips. Let my vindication come from Your presence; Let Your eyes look on the things that are upright. You have tested my heart; You have visited me in the night; You have tried me and have found nothing; I have purposed that my mouth shall not transgress concerning the works of men, by the word of Your lips, I have kept away from the paths of the destroyer. Uphold my steps in Your paths, That my footsteps may not slip. I have called upon You, for You will hear me, O God; incline Your ear to me, and hear my speech. Show your marvelous lovingkindness by Your right hand, O you who save those who trust in You from those who rise up against them.

King David's vindication and restoration came through his faith in God, evidenced by him heeding and obeying the Counsel of God.

Although David lived a fiery trial, the LORD showed Himself mighty and strong on behalf of His chosen king. But take note, it was the fiery trial that gave God the opportunity to prove King David's faith and loyalty to God. The fiery trial was also an opportunity for God to prove His covenant loyalty to David. The trials and testing of David also provided God an opportunity to show His covenant faithfulness to the nation.

As you seek, obtain and obey the Counsel of the LORD for your recovery remember, your recovery is God's recovery. Your vindication is God's vindication. Determine to be like David—seek and obey the Counsel of God for every decision and every battle. Determine in your heart to partner with God to recover all that God has shown you for your restoration. Consider these encouraging words King David penned once the LORD delivered him from the hands of all his enemies and from the hands of Saul:

> I will love you, O LORD, my strength. The LORD is my rock and my fortress and my deliverer; My God, my strength, in whom I will trust; My shield and the horn of my salvation, my stronghold. I will call upon the LORD who is worthy to be praised; So shall I be saved from my enemies. The pangs of death surrounded me, and the floods of ungodliness made me afraid. The sorrows of Sheol surrounded me; the snares of death confronted me. In my distress I called upon the LORD, and cried out to my God; He heard my voice from His temple, and my cry came before Him, even to His ears. Then the earth shook and trembled; the foundations of the hills also quaked and were shaken, Because He was angry. Smoke went up from His nostrils, and devouring fire from His mouth; Coals were kindled by it. He bowed the heavens also, and came down; With darkness under His feet. And He rode upon a cherub, and flew; He flew upon the wings of the wind. He made darkness His secret place; His canopy around Him was dark waters and thick clouds of the skies. From the brightness before Him, His thick clouds passed with hailstones and coals of fire. The LORD thundered from heaven, And the Most High uttered His voice, hailstones and coals of fire. He sent out His arrows and scattered the foe, lightings in abundance and He vanquished them. Then the channels of the sea were seen, the foundations of the world were uncovered. At Your rebuke, O LORD, at the blast of the breath of Your nostrils. He sent from above, he took me; He drew me out of many waters. He delivered me from my strong enemy, from those who hated me, for they were too strong for

me. They confronted me in the day of my calamity, But the LORD was my support. He also brought me out into a broad place; He delivered me because He delighted in me. The LORD rewarded me according to my righteousness; According to the cleanness of my hands He has recompenses me. For I have kept the ways of the LORD, and have not wickedly departed from my God. For all His judgments were before me, and I did not put away His statutes from me. I was also blameless before Him, And I kept myself from my iniquity. Therefore the LORD has recompensed me according to my righteousness, According to the cleanness of my hands in His sight.

—PSALM 18:1-24

$\mathscr{I}$SAIAH 58 FAST: THE KEY TO RESTORATION

$\mathscr{I}$ began the discipline of fasting in 1994. However, it was more than six years of developing this discipline before I gained an understanding of the connection between fasting and restoration. I read, studied, re-read and studied Isaiah Chapter 58 and found it to be the model of an effectual fast. Fasting, according to Chapter 58 will destroy the negative conditions outlined by the prophet in Isaiah Chapter 59 and birth Divine Restoration.

Chapter 58 provides three requirements for restoration: prayer (seeking God), fasting (repentance) and alms giving (giving to the poor). Fasting with prayer, repentance and alms giving is likened to a "three stranded cord that is not easily broken."[62]

While writing this book, I came across a book written by Brad H. Young and called *Meet the Rabbis, Rabbinic Thought and the Teachings*

---

62. Ecclesiastes 4:12

of Jesus. Young dedicated a portion of a chapter in his book to "Rabbinic Teaching on Charity, Prayer and Fasting." Interestingly, Young asserts that prayer, fasting and giving to the poor cancels out decrees of destruction. Young refers to the Jerusalem Talmud, a legal codification that was published in the early Byzantine period (324-610 C.E.), which states that charity, prayer and fasting nullify a harsh decree from heaven.[63] Young writes that, according to a known Rabbi, Rabbi Leazar, a harsh decree may be averted through prayer, righteousness (alms giving) and repentance (fasting). The Scripture found in 2 Chronicles 7:14 was the basis for this Rabbinic thought and declares, "If My people, who are called by My name, will humble themselves and pray and seek My face and turn from their wicked ways, then will I hear from heaven and will forgive their sin and will heal their land."

In the late 1990s, God began to give me understanding concerning fasting and its connection with cancelling negative decrees or decrees of destruction issued in the earth by spiritual and governmental leaders as well as individuals in rebellion to God.[64] As an attorney, the concept of a person issuing an unrighteous decree was not difficult to understand. Yet, the adverse spiritual effects of unrighteous decrees are rarely taught, nor generally understood.

Unrighteous decrees are barriers to the manifestation of God's Counsel in Earth. Unrighteous decrees or edicts made by individuals or by those in authority (political leaders, religious leaders, educational leaders, lawyers, judges, physicians, economic leaders, parents and teachers) weave webs which create barriers to restoration. Unrighteous decrees direct misfortune. Unrighteous decrees rob you of the good plans the LORD has for you. Unrighteous decrees are often conceived

---

63. y.Ta'anit 65b, ch. 2, Hal.1

64. Isaiah 10:2

in the dark secret places of the heart and uttered out of the mouth, thereby creating destruction in Earth.

The Psalmist says:

> For the wicked boasts of his heart's desire; he blesses the greedy and renounces the LORD. The wicked in his proud countenance does not seek God; God is in none of his thoughts. His ways are always prospering; Your judgments are far above, out of his sight; as for all his enemies, he sneers at them. He has said in his heart, "I shall not be moved; I shall never be in adversity." His mouth is full of cursing and deceit and oppression; Under his tongue is trouble and iniquity. He sits in the lurking places of the villages; In the secret places he murders the innocent; His eyes are *secretly* fixed on the helpless. He lies in wait secretly, as a lion in his den; He lies in wait to catch the poor; he catches the poor when he draws him into his net.
>
> —PSALM 10:3-9

> For look! The wicked bend their bow, they make ready their arrow on the string, that they may shoot secretly at the upright in heart.
>
> —PSALM 11:2

In the post-exilic book of Esther, a destructive decree was formed in the heart of a jealous and envious man named Haman, the son of Hammedatha the Agagite.[65] Haman was not an insignificant man; he was considered an executive, a prince above all princes in the land of Persia, the ruling nation on Earth. Because Mordecai, a Jew, would not bow to him, it brought wrath to Haman's heart.[66] It was Haman's

---

65. Esther 3:1
66. Esther 3:5

unrighteous wrath that caused him to seek to annihilate all the Jews living in the kingdom of Ahasuerus.[67]

To accomplish his plan, Haman used his position to obtain from the king an *unrighteous decree aimed at destroying* all Jews living in the kingdom.[68] After the Jews learned of the decree, they fasted and prayed.[69] After they fasted and prayed, God miraculously caused the decree to be aborted and nullified, with no loss of life to the Jews.[70]

The prophet Isaiah addressed unrighteous decrees issued by government and religious leaders and declared the demise of leaders who had made it a practice of issuing unrighteous decrees against the poor, *thereby promoting misfortune and injustices*:

> Woe to those who decree unrighteous decrees, who write misfortune, which they have prescribed to rob the needy of justice, and to take what is right from the poor of My people, that widows may be their prey, and that they may rob the fatherless.
>
> What will you do in the day of punishment, and in the desolation which will come from afar? To whom will you flee for help? And where will you leave your glory?
>
> —ISAIAH 10:1-4

King Nebuchadnezzar, a Babylonian king, was also enticed to issue a destructive decree aimed at the prophet Daniel and his three friends. The king had previously issued an edict that required all those in his kingdom to bow down and worship a golden image. Those who did

---

67. Esther 3:6
68. Esther 3:8-15
69. Esther 4:16
70. Esther 7:10

not bow would be cast into a furnace.[71] Daniel and his three Hebrew friends refused to bow to the golden image and were sent by decree into the furnace.[72] However, the LORD appeared with them in the midst of the furnace, and the four were seen "walking in the midst of the fire." When King Nebuchadnezzar saw these men on whose bodies the fire had no power, he blessed God.[73]

Years later King Darius, another Babylonian king, was enticed to issue a destructive decree aimed at Daniel.[74] This time the decree declared that if anyone petitioned any god or man for thirty days except for King Darius, the person would be cast into a den of lions.[75] Daniel continued to pray to God three times a day and, therefore, according to the decree, was sentenced to the lion's den. In this account, King Darius fasted for Daniel. After Daniel was put in the lion's den, God sent an angel and shut the lion's mouth so that it did not hurt Daniel.[76]

These Scriptures highlight various unrighteous decrees issued by individuals in authority aimed at destroying individuals and people groups. Yet, these Scriptures also summarize the various ways the LORD sovereignly intervened to nullify the adverse effects of the destructive decrees.

The Scripture also teaches that God will even cancel a *righteous* decree of judgment against a nation, when a nation or people group humble themselves, seek repentance and fast and pray. The Old Testament book of Jonah outlines how fasting and prayer cancelled a righteous decree

---

71. Daniel 3:10-11
72. Daniel 3:23
73. Daniel 3:19-28
74. Daniel 6
75. Daniel 6:7
76. Daniel 6:22

of judgment issued from heaven against the Assyrian city of Nineveh. The prophet Jonah proclaimed to the city that God would overthrow the city in 40 days if the city did not repent.[77] The people of Nineveh proclaimed a fast, and when the word of Jonah reached the king, the king issued a citywide proclamation of fasting, prayer and repentance. The Scripture states,

> God saw their works that they turned from their evil way; and God relented from the disaster that He had said He would bring upon them, and He did not do it.
>
> —JONAH 3:10

The book of Jonah provides clear evidence that fasting and repentant prayer can and will garner the attention of heaven and move God to change His mind and cancel even a righteously issued decree of judgment.

What about alms giving? What does the Scripture say about how God responds to the giving of alms with fasting and prayer? Through fasting, prayer and alms giving, Cornelius, a Gentile centurion was visited by an Angel of the LORD who declared to him that "his prayers and alms have come up before God as a memorial."[78] In response to this devout, yet unbelieving man's prayers, fasting and alms giving, God gave the Apostle Peter a vision and sent him to declare to Cornelius and his household the way of salvation.[79]

Proverbs 19:17 declares that when we are kind to the poor we lend to the LORD, and "He will reward him for what he has done." When we

---

77. Jonah 3:3
78. Acts 10:1-4, 30
79. Acts 10:9-48

give to the poor, it becomes a memorial before God, and we store up an account in heaven. The earthly benefits of this heavenly account are seen through these promises given by the LORD:

> God saw their works that they turned from their evil way; and God relented from the disaster that He had said He would bring upon them, and He did not do it.
>
> —JONAH 3:10

A profound concept regarding the poor is found in Jewish thought. It holds that a person sees God's face or beholds the face of God through doing righteousness by giving alms to the poor. This thought is seemingly affirmed in the words of the LORD when He declared that when you give food and drink to hungry and thirsty brethren, you are giving food and drink to God:

> When the Son of Man comes in His glory, and all the holy angels with Him, then He will sit on the throne of His glory. All the nations will be gathered before Him and He will separate them one from another, as a shepherd divides his sheep from the goats. And He will set the sheep on His right hand, but the goats on the left. Then the King will say to those on His right hand, "Come, you blessed of My Father, inherit the kingdom prepared for you from the foundations of the world; for I was hungry and you gave Me food; I was thirsty and you gave Me drink; I was a stranger and you took Me in; I was naked and you clothed Me; I was sick and you visited Me; I was in prison and you came to Me."
>
> Then the righteous will answer Him, saying, "Lord, when did we see You hungry and feed You, or thirsty and give You drink? When did we see You a stranger and take You in, or naked and clothe You?" And the King will answer and say to them,

"Assuredly, I say to you, in as much as you did it to one of the least of these My brethren, you did it to Me."

—MATTHEW 25:31-40

Fasting, prayer and giving to the poor are acts of righteousness, and righteousness makes you bold as a lion:

The wicked flee when no one pursues, but the righteous are bold as a lion.

—PROVERBS 28:1

I recall one day while fasting and praying I heard the Holy Spirit say, "You have no idea the power of your prayers in heaven." The Scripture says, "The effective and fervent prayers of the righteous man avails much."[80] Effective and fervent prayers of the righteous pierce the realms of darkness and nullify unrighteous decrees aimed at hindering the fulfillment of God's Counsel in your life.

GOD'S INSTRUCTIONS FOR A FAST

God's instructions for an effectual fast, a fast intended by God to lead to restoration, are found in Isaiah Chapter 58:

Cry loudly, do not hold back; raise your voice like a trumpet, and declare to My people their transgression, and to the house of Jacob their sins. Yet they seek Me day by day, and delight to know My ways, as a nation that has done righteousness, and has not forsaken the ordinances of their God. They ask Me for just decisions, they delight in the nearness of God. Why have we

---

80. James 5:16

fasted and Thou dost not see? Why have we humbled ourselves and Thou dost not notice?

Behold, on the day of your fast you find your desire, and drive hard all your workers, behold you fast for contention and strife and to strike with a wicked fist. You do not fast like you do today to make your voice heard on high. "Is it a fast like this which I choose, a day for a man to humble himself? Is it for bowing one's head like a reed, and for spreading out sackcloth and ashes as a bed? Will you call this a fast, even an acceptable day to the LORD?

Is this not the fast which I have chosen, to loose the bonds of wickedness, to undo the bands of the yoke, and to let the oppressed go free, and break every yoke? Is it not to divide your bread with the hungry and bring the homeless poor into the house; When you see the naked to cover him; and not to hide yourself from your own flesh. Then your light will break out like the dawn, and your recovery will speedily spring forth; and your righteousness will go before you; the glory of the LORD will be your rear guard. Then you will call and the LORD will answer; You will cry, and He will say, 'Here I am.'"

If you remove the yoke from your midst, the pointing of the finger and speaking wickedness, and if you give yourself to the hungry, and satisfy the desire of the afflicted, then your light will rise in darkness, and your gloom will become like midday. The LORD will continually guide you, and satisfy your desire in scorched places, and give strength to your bones, and you will be like a watered garden, and like a spring of water whose waters do not fail. And those from among you will rebuild the ancient ruins, you will raise up the age-old foundations, and you will be called the Repairer of the Breach, the Restorer of the Streets in which to Dwell.

If because of the Sabbath, you turn your foot from doing your own pleasure on My holy day and call the Sabbath a delight, the holy day of the LORD honorable, and shall honor it, desisting from your own ways, from seeking your own pleasure, and speaking your own words, then you will take delight in the LORD, and I will make you ride on the heights of the earth; and I will feed you with the heritage of Jacob your father, for the mouth of the LORD has spoken.

The entire chapter of Isaiah 58 concerns instructions given to Jewish exiles who had returned to Canaan after completing seventy years in captivity. At that time, the city of Jerusalem was in ruins—there was no temple, no central place of worship and no king. The instructions given were to restore the land and restore true worship. It was also the answer to the question of the people, "Why had the promised restoration been delayed?"

Isaiah begins the chapter by stating that the delay was not due to God but was due to their own sin. Their fasting, which was done regularly, was not in accordance with a fast that pleased God. Although the remnant knew how to abstain from food and knew how to inquire of God for the making of just and equitable decisions, the actions and intents of their hearts were not in accordance with justice.

Although the people had an outward appearance of spiritual desire and ambition to "know God and seek His ways,"[81] there existed an internal problem—a heart of rebellion to God.

Isaiah begins by telling the people their transgressions, the sins that held up the promised restoration. The sins identified by the prophet include:

---

81. Isaiah 58:2

1. fasting to find your own pleasure;

2. exploiting wage earnings;

3. fasting for strife and debate;

4. striking with the fist of wickedness;

5. fasting to be seen and have your voice heard.

Isaiah pronounced the fatal flaw with the people's fast—they had turned the fast day into a day of self-centeredness and a day to earn a benefit through exploiting wage earners with toilsome work. The fast that was intended by God to bring about justice and peace among brethren ended in fighting and strife. Why the list of these sins? Because, all the sins identified are directly related to the first and foremost commandment given by God to the nation:

> Love the Lord your God with all your heart, mind, soul and strength and love your neighbor as yourself.
>
> —LEVITICUS 19:18, DEUTERONOMY 6: 5

In v. 6, Isaiah declares the purpose of a true and acceptable fast, what God was looking for from His covenant people:

1. To lose the bonds of wickedness;

2. To undue heavy burdens;

3. To let the oppressed go free;

4. That you break every yoke;

5. That you share your bread with the hungry;

6. That you bring to your house the poor who are cast out;

7. When you see the naked that you cover him and not hide yourself from your own flesh;

8. That you take away the yoke from your midst, the pointing of the finger and speaking wickedness;

9. That you extend your soul to the hungry and satisfy the afflicted soul;

10. That you turn away your foot from the Sabbath and from doing your pleasure on My holy day and call the Sabbath a delight, the holy day of the LORD honorable.

Nine of ten "desires" of the LORD can be carved down to one statement:

An acceptable fast is one in which man comes into conformity with God's thoughts on how man should treat his fellow man. However, rather than justice and peace being the dominate relational motive in the nation, perversity prevailed. Hear what the prophet Ezekiel has to say:

> The iniquity of the house of Israel and Judah is exceedingly great, and the land is full of bloodshed and the city full of perversity; for they say, "The LORD has forsaken the land, and the LORD does not see!"
>
> —EZEKIEL 9:9

The word for "perversity" used by the prophet is the Hebrew word *mutteh,* which means distortion. It is a word derived from the root meaning to stretch, to incline or to bend and is used by Isaiah to describe the perverseness of the nation in distorting God's laws and justice. Perversion had entered the nation through the people departing from God, through speaking oppression and revolt against God and denying His commandments. These actions were the cause of the web of lies that covered the nation and the people and the cause God's hand of deliverance was stayed:

> For our transgressions are multiplied before You, and our sins testify against us; For our transgressions are with us; And as for our iniquities, we know them: In transgressing and lying against the LORD, and departing from our God, speaking oppression and revolt, conceiving and uttering from the heart words of falsehood.
>
> —ISAIAH 59:12-13

The Hebrew word for "transgression" in Isaiah 59 is the word *pasha* and means to rebel or revolt against God. In revolting and rebelling against God, all truth is laid aside. The result was lies and error, crookedness and perversions. In this condition, the land became defiled and the people became filled with crookedness and perversion in thought, action and deed. Justice was turned back, righteousness stood afar off, truth fell in the street, and equity—the balancing of just scales— could not enter.[82]

The fast designed by God was for the nation's spiritual and governmental leaders, as well as the people, to return in their heart to God so that correction could be made to these conditions. The fast was to eliminate the means and avenues, veins and arteries, of social and government mismanagement that had caused people to be placed under heavy and oppressive burdens. It was designed to untie and reverse unrighteous decrees, edicts and law decisions that had caused injustices to abound. The fast was designed to penetrate, destroy and remove unrighteous structures that had produced oppression of the

---

82. Isaiah 59:14-15

poor and needy in society, the class of people specifically called by the nation to protect through the execution of justice.

The prophet Zechariah reminds us that wrath came to the nation of Israel, and the nation was "scattered like a whirlwind among the nations" because they failed to heed the words of the LORD to execute true justice and for everyone to show mercy and compassion to his brother:

> Then the word of the LORD came to Zechariah, saying, Thus says the LORD of hosts: "Execute true justice, show mercy and compassion, everyone to his brother. Do not oppress the widow or the fatherless, the alien or the poor. Let none of you plan evil in his heart against his brother."
>
> But they refused to heed, shrugged their shoulders, and stopped their ears so that they could not hear.
>
> Yes, they made their hearts like flint, refusing to hear the law and the words which the LORD of hosts had sent by his Spirit through the former prophets. Thus great wrath came from the LORD of hosts.
>
> Therefore it happened, that just as He proclaimed, and they would not hear, so they called out and "I would not listen," says the LORD of hosts.
>
> "But I scattered them with a whirlwind among all the nations which they had not known. Thus the land became desolate after them, so that no one passed through or returned; for they made the pleasant land desolate."
>
> —ZECHARIAH 7:8-10

If done sincerely and honestly, a fast designed by God would garner heaven's attention for the removal of every barrier erected by man and allow God's hand of restoration to be released. The LORD declared that if the nation would do God's righteousness and heed His moral commands, if the people would cease from oppressing the poor, cease from pointing the finger and speaking wickedness by falsely slandering and accusing their brethren, and if they would observe the Sabbath with pure and joyful worship then the covenant-making, covenant-keeping God, would give light, healing and a full and speedy recovery to the land.[83]

The restoration pronounced is all encompassing and includes the following covenant promises:

1. Your light will break forth like the morning (new beginnings);

2. Your healing will spring forth speedily (personal restoration);

3. Your righteousness shall go before you and the glory of the Lord will be your rear guard (security before and behind);

4. You will call, and the LORD will answer; you will cry, and He will say, "Here I am" (unbroken relationship with the Lord);

5. Your light shall dawn in the darkness, and your darkness shall be as the noonday; the LORD will guide you continually (clear direction), satisfy your soul in drought and strengthen your bones (renewal and strength);

6. You will be like a watered garden, like a spring of water, whose waters do not fail (continual resources);

7. Those from among you will build the old waste places, you shall raise up the foundations of many generations; you shall be called the Repairer of the Breach, the Restorer of Streets to Dwell In (divine restoration from past disaster);

---

83. Isaiah 58:8-9

8. Then you shall delight yourself in the LORD, and I will cause you to ride on the high heels of the earth and feed you with the heritage of Jacob your father.

—ISAIAH 58:8-14

The LORD's instructions are specific and direct: repent of rebellion and lying to God and conform your ways to the way of true righteousness. When you do, your healing will spring forth speedily.

The word "healing" used in Isaiah 58 is the Hebrew word *aruwkâh,* which means the healing of a wound, restoration and repair. It also means restoring to soundness, wholeness and health. The intuitive meaning is healing caused by growth of new flesh over a wound.

Isaiah begins his oracle with an accounting of the sins that were separating the people from the thoughts and plans of God yet ends his oracle with the blessings awaiting the people upon a heart reform. The instructions given were for success and not for calamity, to give the people a future and a hope.[84] When the LORD's Counsel was heeded, the fast would invoke the immediate and sure attention of Israel's covenant-keeping God and the intended restoration in their lives and land would ensue.

ISAIAH 58 IS A MODEL FOR TODAY

Instructions in righteousness given to Isaiah hold equally true for us today and for every nation on the earth. Isaiah 58 provides the model of an acceptable fast, for righteous living and the remedy to move God's hand of restoration. It is a fast I have found to be true time and time again. As I pursue the instructions found in Isaiah 58, I have witnessed

---

84. Jeremiah 29:11

the removal of oppressive yokes and the nullifying of unrighteous decrees. I have witnessed the removal of webs covering individuals, people groups and even cities. Once removed, a pathway was made for the Holy Spirit to enter in and bring "times of refreshing," healing to hearts, minds, bodies and relationships. Refreshing makes the barren lands begin to bear fruit.

I have witnessed destructive decrees reversed,[85] covenants of death nullified,[86] family heritages restored and salvation spring forth from the earth.[87] Through an Isaiah 58 fast, I have witnessed the fulfillment of Isaiah 40:4-5:

> Every valley shall be exalted and every mountain and hill brought low; the crooked places shall be made straight and the rough places smooth; the glory of the LORD shall be revealed, and all flesh shall see it together; for the mouth of the LORD has spoken.

Isaiah 40:4-5 portrays a time when the lowly are exalted, the proud are brought low, and the things that had once been crooked are now made straight. It is on this straight road that the King of Glory, the LORD, can enter. When this occurs, God's righteousness will pour from heaven onto the earth, and the earth will respond by bringing forth the fruits of salvation and righteousness.[88]

Yahweh, the covenant-keeping, covenant-fulfilling God, is true to every jot and tittle of His Word.[89] If we will seek God and seek to

---

85. Isaiah 10:22
86. Isaiah 28:18
87. Isaiah 45:8
88. Isaiah 45:8
89. Matthew 5:18

conform our ways to His ways of righteousness, we can experience the glorious results of restoration. Isaiah 55: 6-7 states,

> Seek the Lord while He may be found, call upon Him while He is near. Let the wicked forsake his way, and the unrighteous man his thoughts; let him return to the LORD, and He will have mercy on him; and to our God, for He will abundantly pardon.
>
> —ISAIAH 55:6-7

God is ready with His infinite mercy to pardon abundantly and remove every negative effect of sin and the aftermath of captivity and destruction. An Isaiah 58 fast is a golden key given to assist in the LORD's *Divine Restoration* plan. I encourage you to consider an Isaiah 58 fast. Take to heart the plethora of restorative promises spoken by Isaiah. The promises are timeless and immutable and are as applicable today as they were over 2700 years ago.

$\mathcal{P}$IERCING REBELLION, DIVINATION AND WITCHCRAFT

"$\mathcal{H}$as the LORD as great delight in burnt offerings and sacrifices, as in obeying the voice of the LORD?

Behold, to obey is better than sacrifice, and to heed than the fat of rams.

For rebellion is as the sin of witchcraft, and stubbornness is as iniquity and idolatry.

Because you have rejected the word of the LORD, He has also rejected you from being king."

—1 SAMUEL 15:22-23

In this account, the prophet Samuel summarizes the judgment announced as a result of King Saul rejecting the word of the LORD.

God had commanded King Saul to destroy the Amalekites. The Scripture states that King Saul transgressed the commandment of the LORD and failed to execute the command because he feared the people and obeyed their voice rather than the voice of God.[90] Because King Saul rejected the word of the LORD, God rejected him from being king.

The word "rebellion" used in 1 Samuel 15:23 is the Hebrew word *mriy* and comes from the word *marah*, which means bitterness. It is a masculine noun meaning obstinacy, stubbornness and rebelliousness. It most often is used to describe a refusal to obey the precepts of God's law.

The word "divination" used in 1 Samuel 15:23 is the Hebrew word *qesem*, which means divine sentence. Divination describes the cultic practice of soothsaying, which is decreeing words of falsehood or false prophesy— words God did not speak. Because our words have power and are the creative force on the earth, when individuals and those in authority rebel against God and speak (divine) words that God did not speak, sentences and judgments are created that God did not authorize. These judgments create walls and barriers that keep out the Counsel of God.

The LORD told the nation of Israel that He was going to direct the nation through true prophets not false prophets or kings who rebelled against God and practiced divination.[91] When we individually or as a nation rebel against God, we are guilty of practicing the sin of witchcraft. When we rebel against God in any area of our lives, we open the door to listening to and speaking words of falsehood and revolt against God. When rebellion occurs, we attract to individuals and leaders whose hearts are also in rebellion to God. These attractions

---

90. 1 Samuel 15:24

91. Deuteronomy 18:9-22

produce ungodly alliances that cause yokes of oppression and webs of lies to be formed that keep out the Counsel of God.

In this place of rebellion, manipulation, control and the domination of others thrive through fear and intimidation. Morality becomes twisted and perverted because lies are promoted as truth. Corruption and faithlessness are found among spiritual and governmental leaders. It is here that the heart of the righteous, which God did not make sad, is made sad.[92]

The prophet Ezekiel spoke about these conditions when both the male and female leaders in Israel were speaking lies about God and decreeing (divining) words of falsehood from their evil hearts. As a result, their words formed "walls of untempered mortar" that suppressed the truth of what God had spoken through His prophets, truth regarding the condition of the nation and truth regarding a dire need for the nation to repent before judgment was issued from heaven. God commanded Ezekiel to prophesy against these walls so that He could remove the walls and bring deliverance to His people.

And the word of the LORD came to me saying,

"Son of man, prophesy against the prophets of Israel who prophesy, and say to those who prophesy out of their own heart, 'Hear the word of the LORD!'"...

Say to those who plaster it with untempered mortar, that it will fall. There will be flooding rain and you, O great hailstones, shall fall; and a stormy wind shall tear it down...

So I will break down the wall you have plastered with untempered mortar, and bring it down to the ground, so that its foundation

---

92. Ezekiel 13:22

will be uncovered; it will fall, and you shall be consumed in the midst of it. Then you shall know that I am the LORD...

"Likewise, son of man, set your face against the daughters of your people, who prophesy out of their own heart; prophesy against them and say,

'Thus says the Lord GOD: "Woe to the women who sew magic charms on the sleeves and make veils for the heads of people of every height to hunt souls! Will you hunt the souls of My people and keep yourselves alive?

And will you profane Me among My people for handfuls of barley and for pieces of bread, killing people who should not die and keeping people alive who should not live, by your lying to My people who listen to lies?'"

Therefore thus says the Lord GOD: "Behold I am against your magic charms by which you hunt souls there like birds. I will tear them from your arms, and let the souls go, the souls you hunt like birds.

I will also tear off your veils and deliver My people out of your hand, and they shall no longer be as prey in your hand. Then you shall know that I am the LORD.

Because with lies you have made the heart of the righteous sad, whom I have not made sad; and you have strengthened the hand of the wicked, so that he does not turn from his wicked way to save his life...

—EZEKIEL 13:1-23

In this account, Ezekiel describes how walls are erected and barriers are formed through the divination of lies. God had sent His prophets to declare to the nation that if the nation did not repent of its rebellion, judgment would ensue. To the contrary, false prophets were divining lies of peace, not judgment. The lies created spiritual barriers and walls to the entry of God's truth. As a result, the heart of the righteous was made sad, whom God had not made sad.

The problem with the nation not receiving and heeding the voice of truth was monumental. If the people failed to receive and heed the voice of truth, they could not seek a pardon through repentance, nor could they begin to prepare their lives for the coming exile and judgment. By listening to lies of peace when there was no peace, the people were given a false hope—a false sense of security—and were left to die behind walls of falsehood.

God commanded Ezekiel to prophesy "against the walls built with untempered mortar" so that God could send flooding rain, hailstones, and a stormy wind to destroy the wall of lies and deliver His people.

Romans 1:18-19 declares that when an individual, Christian or non-Christian chooses to act in unrighteousness and wickedness through tongue or deed, that person suppresses, pushes down, withholds and covers up truth found in the knowledge of God:

> For the wrath of God is revealed from heaven against all ungodliness and unrighteousness of men, who suppress the truth in unrighteousness, because what may be known of God is manifest in them, for God has shown it to them.
>
> —ROMANS 1:18-19

MAN'S UNRIGHTEOUS COUNSEL KEEPS OUT GOD'S RIGHTEOUS COUNSEL

It is indisputable that unrighteous actions and disobedience to God suppresses, covers up and pushes down truth from manifesting on Earth toward you, your family and your nation. Unrighteous actions keep out God's righteous actions. Unrighteous thoughts keep out God's righteous thoughts.

An Isaiah 58 fast is God's solution to this problem. An Isaiah 58 fast will cause your will to come into alignment with God's will. When this alignment happens, you can pierce the unseen realms of rebellion, divination and witchcraft that have kept you from experiencing the LORD's justice, righteousness, truth and equity.

Ask God to reveal where rebellion may have been secretly hidden in your life. It may be something you were involved in years ago or a lifestyle you lived previously in rebellion to God. Rebellion may have come through alliances you made as a Christian with individuals whose hearts were secretly in rebellion to God. Whatever the case may be, an Isaiah 58 fast is designed to both reveal and destroy areas of rebellion, divination and witchcraft which have suppressed truth in your life.

During your fast, ask God to reveal any past or current unrighteous alliances you have engaged in and any unrighteous words decreed, or unrighteous deeds done. Ask God to reveal all pacts, covenants or agreements made knowingly or unknowingly with words of death or destruction. Ask God to reveal any pacts, covenants or agreements made with any social or religious groups that promote death and destruction, not life and peace.

Any covenants (oaths, pacts, pledges) made with fraternal orders, entities, organizations and societies should be spiritually scrutinized. If any covenant and allegiance does not align with the Word of God, you may have unknowingly made an unrighteous alliance to an organization or association. These covenants cause a divided allegiance to God, no matter what religious words are used as part of the pact or agreement. You cannot pledge allegiance to God and pledge allegiance to man.

During your fast, ask the LORD to reveal any divided alliances or allegiances you may have knowingly or unknowingly made, including pledging allegiances to fraternal organizations, societies or associations.

Fasting is also a time to renounce, reject and disclaim any agreements made with occult practices. It is a time to renounce, reject and disclaim all counsel you have knowingly or unknowing entertained through horoscopes, palm-readers, spiritualist, shaman and spirit guides. If you don't renounce connections and agreements made with these unrighteous alliances, the agreements will remain in the unseen realm of the spirit and will hinder the restoration God intends to bring to your life.

You must choose to follow the Counsel of God found in His Word. God alone is the source of all wisdom and truth. Psalm 19 outlines the benefits of the Word of God. It converts the soul, makes wise the simple, rejoices the heart, enlightens the eyes and is more to be desired than gold:

> "The law of the LORD is perfect converting the soul;
>
> The testimony of the LORD is sure, making wise the simple;
> The statutes of the LORD are right, rejoicing the heart;
>
> The commandment of the LORD is pure, enlightening the eyes;
>
> The fear of the LORD is clean, enduring forever;
>
> The judgments of the LORD are true and righteous altogether.
>
> More to be desired are they than gold, Yes, than much fine gold;
>
> Sweeter also than honey and the honeycomb.
>
> Moreover by them your servant is warned, and in keeping them there is great reward."
>
> —PSALM 19:7-11

The prophet Elijah asked the nation of Israel to make a choice between worshiping God or worshiping the Canaanite and Phoenician deity

Baal.[93] At that time, the nation had been under a severe water drought, prophesized by Elijah.[94] The drought was a curse, not a blessing, and was imposed as a result of King Ahab and his wife, Queen Jezebel, allowing the worship of Baal alongside the worship of Yahweh. At the end of the divine sentence, God told Elijah to call the nation together at Mount Carmel for a showdown between the 450 false prophets of Baal and God's true prophet Elijah. During this encounter, God wanted to prove that He alone is the One true God; therefore, He alone deserves sincere and undivided devotion.

When the prophets of Baal gathered on Mount Carmel, they built an altar and called on their god to answer their offering by fire, but no answer came. When it was Elijah's turn, he first repaired the altar of the LORD that was broken down (symbolic of preparing the altar of the heart where worship takes place) and then took twelve stones according to the number of the tribes of Israel and offered a sacrifice to God. The Scripture declares the following account of God's answer to Elijah's prayer:

> And it came to pass, at the time of the offering of the evening sacrifice, that Elijah the prophet came near and said, "LORD God of Abraham, Isaac and Israel, let it be known this day that You are God in Israel and I am Your servant, and that I have done all these things at Your word.
>
> Hear me, O LORD, hear me, that this people may know that You are the LORD God, and that You have turned their hearts back to You again."

---

93. 1 Kings 18
94. 1 Kings 17:1

> Then the fire of the LORD fell and consumed the burnt sacrifice, and the wood and the stones and the dust, and it licked up the altar that was in the trench.
>
> Now when all the people saw it, they fell on their faces; and they said, "The LORD, He is God! The LORD, He is God!"
>
> —1 KINGS 18:36-39

After Elijah's prayer, fire was sent from heaven and consumed Elijah's offering, showing the spectators that the LORD alone could answer by fire; therefore, He alone should be worshiped. After this encounter, the nation turned their hearts back to God, and the drought ended.

Ask the LORD to reveal any seeds of rebellion living in the heart that would cause you to turn away from God or cause you to justify a divided allegiance or devotion to God. One of my favorite Scriptures is found in Psalm 139. In this Scripture, the Psalmist asks God to put his heart on trial:

> Search me, O God, and know my heart; try me, and know my anxieties; and see if there is any wicked way in me, and lead me in the way everlasting.
>
> —PSALM 139:33-34

Ask the LORD to put your heart on trial—to evaluate it. I pray this Scripture often asking the Holy Spirit to show me any conflicts in my motives and intentions and to reveal any divided allegiances in my heart. Remember, a man cannot serve two masters (Matthew 6:24). Divided alliances will produce ill will, contempt, resentment and unforgiveness toward God and others.

Ask the LORD to reveal unrighteous attitudes toward your brother and neighbor, hidden attitudes of strife, envy, jealousy and competition with other Christians and non-Christians. Ask the LORD to reveal unrighteous judgments made from your mouth due to unrighteous anger, pride and arrogance. All these sins should be confessed.

The prophet Malachi declared that only after the refining fire of the LORD purifies our hearts can we offer the LORD an offering in righteousness, an offering that is pleasing to Him.[95]

> But who can endure the day of His coming? And who can stand when He appears? For He is like a refiner's fire and like launderers' soap.
>
> He will sit as refiner and a purifier of silver; He will purify the sons of Levi, and purge them as gold and silver, that they may offer to the LORD an offering in righteousness.
>
> *Then* the offering of Judah and Jerusalem will be pleasant to the LORD, as in the days of old, as in the former years. "And I will come near you for judgment; I will be a swift witness against sorcerers, against adulterers, against perjurers, against those who exploit wage earners and widows and orphans, and against those who turn away an alien because they do not fear Me," says the LORD of hosts.
>
> —MALACHI 3:2-5

This Scripture explains that once we offer God an offering in righteousness, then the LORD will be a witness against sorcerers, adulterers and perjurers and against those who exploit wage earners, widows and orphans. Not until our hands are clean and our hearts

---

95. Malachi 3:3

have been purified can we expect the hand of the LORD to be a witness against those who practice divination and stubbornly oppose, rebel and suppress truth.

Fasting is a time to allow the LORD's refining fire to touch your heart. It is a time to cultivate a heart of sincere devotion to God. Devotion to God means to devote yourself to be like God—to think like Him and act like Him. Ephesians 5:1 says, "Therefore be imitators of God as dear children."

Fasting is a time to seek cleansing from all filthiness of the flesh and to perfect holiness in the fear of God.[96] It is a time to seek the removal of strongholds in your heart and mind that have resisted, rebelled and opposed the knowledge of God, His laws, His commandments, His statutes and His judgments. Simply put, fasting is a time to ask God to reveal and remove thoughts and attitudes you, your family and past generations have developed (knowingly or unknowingly) that have opposed the royal law of love.

Finally, an acceptable fast will bring about a change of heart and mind that will allow you to effectively pierce realms of rebellion, divination and witchcraft that have kept you from experiencing the manifestation of the Counsel of God in your life and in your circumstances. Once these high places are removed, justice, righteousness, truth and equity can flow unhindered in your life.

GO AND LEARN

The prophet Micah was a contemporary with the prophet Isaiah in the eighth century. He lived during a time when the nation of Israel suffered from faithless leaders. In his declarations, he pronounced

---

96. 2 Corinthians 7:1

a legal complaint brought by the LORD against the nation, but in conclusion told the people what was required of them by the LORD:

For the LORD has a complaint against His people, and He will contend with Israel.

"O My people, what have I done to you? And how have I wearied you? Testify against Me.

For I brought you up from the land of Egypt, I redeemed you from the house of bondage; and I sent before you Moses, Aaron, and Miriam.

O My people, remember now, what Balak king of Moab counseled, and what Balaam the son of Beor answered him, from Acacia Grove to Gilgal, that you may know the righteousness of the LORD."

With what shall I come before the LORD, and bow myself before the High God? Shall I come before Him with burnt offerings, with calves a year old?

Will the LORD be pleased with thousands of rams, ten thousand rivers of oil? Shall I give my firstborn for my transgression, the fruit of my body for the sin of my soul?

Has He shown you, O man, what is good: and what does the LORD require of you but to do justly, to love mercy and to walk humbly with your God?

—MICAH 6:2B-8

The word "mercy" used by Micah is the Hebrew word *chesed* which means kindness, unfailing love, tenderness and faithfulness. It is most often associated in Scripture with God's mercy.

Jesus Christ, in quoting the prophet Hosea,[97] who also used the word *chesed*, declared to the religious leaders in Jerusalem what they should *go and learn*:

> As Jesus passed on from there, He saw a man named Matthew sitting at the tax office. And He said to him, "Follow Me." So he arose and followed Him.
>
> Now it happened as Jesus sat at the table in the house, that behold, many tax collectors and sinners came and sat down with Him and His disciples.
>
> And when the Pharisees saw it, they said to his disciples, "Why does your Teacher eat with tax collectors and sinners?"
>
> When Jesus heard that, He said to them, "Those who are well have no need of a physician, but those who are sick. But go and learn what this means: 'I desire mercy and not sacrifice.' For I did not come to call the righteous but sinners to repentance."
>
> —MATTHEW 9:9-13

If the LORD told the religious leaders who understood and taught the law of God to *go and learn* what God meant when He said, "I desire mercy and not sacrifice," how much more of a responsibility do we have to do likewise? During an Isaiah 58 fast, we should sincerely *go and learn* what God means when He said, "I desire mercy and not sacrifice."

During your fast, ask the LORD to reveal and remove all barriers and obstructions in your mind and heart that have hindered the flow of God's mercy in you and through you toward others. The Greek word for "desire" in Matthew 9:9-13 is the word *thelo* and means to will, to have in mind, to purpose, intend or be pleased. It is the LORD's will,

---

97. Hosea 6:6

intent and purpose—it is what will please the LORD—if we will go and learn His mercy.

The LORD declares the heaviest or weightiest matter of the law of God is justice, mercy and faith. In Matthew 23, Jesus Christ speaks to the religious leaders and declares seven "woes" as He issued His righteous indictment: the people had an outward form of religion, but no true spirituality. Like the prophet Isaiah described, the leaders placed outward burdens, regulations and ordinances on the people too heavy for them to bear. While professing an outward righteousness, the leaders were unjust in their conduct toward each other. Three of these "woes" are outlined here:

> "Woe to you, scribes and Pharisees, hypocrites! For you pay tithe of mint and anise and cumin, and have neglected the weightier matters of the law: justice and mercy and faith. These you ought to have done, without leaving the others undone.
>
> Blind guides, who strain at a gnat and swallow a camel!
>
> Woe to you, scribes and Pharisees, hypocrites! For you cleanse the outside of the cup and dish, but inside they are full of extortion and self-indulgence.
>
> Blind Pharisee, first cleanse the inside of the cup and dish, that the outside of them may be clean also.
>
> Woe to you, scribes and Pharisees, hypocrites! For you are like whitewashed tombs which indeed appear beautiful outwardly, but inside are full of dead men's bones and all uncleanness.
>
> Even so you also outwardly appear righteous, to men, but inside you are full of hypocrisy and lawlessness."
>
> —MATTHEW 23:23-28

Isaiah 58 and Matthew 23 announce the plan of God—a change of the heart. God wants our hearts to be made like His heart, a heart of mercy toward each other.

Fasting with repentance is a divine formula to have mercy formed and fashioned in your heart. When you seek mercy toward others, God responds by identifying and removing barriers that have previously held back the flow of God's mercy toward you. In Matthew 5:7, the LORD said, "Blessed are the merciful, for they shall obtain mercy." The word for "mercy" used here is the Greek word *eleemon* and means to have active mercy and compassion, to have these tendencies with a corresponding action.

Fasting, according to Isaiah 58, can be likened to a fiery, double-edged sword that pierces the unseen realms of rebellion, divination and witchcraft, which have held up the flow of God's mercy to you and through you and have kept you from experiencing times of refreshing.

THE POWER OF AN ISAIAH 58 FAST

A friend wanted to join me in an Isaiah 58 fast. During the fast, she sought repentance and began to experience personal restoration as well as restoration in her family and business. She also began to witness the Spirit of God move in the congregation she was attending with many people receiving Jesus Christ as their Lord and Savior.

During the fast, oppression that had bound her business due to a former personal and business relationship was revealed and destroyed. After the oppression was removed, her business began to thrive. With no money spent on advertising or marketing, the business increased in favor as evidenced by a marked increase in sales, satisfied customers writing reviews on various Internet sites and the local media granting facetime and attention to the business. An Isaiah 58 fast will reveal and destroy yokes of oppression and spiritual barriers that have been erected to keep you from experiencing the LORD's good plans and purposes.

As a result of a fast, I have witnessed the Word of God that was never read before being studied in Bible study groups, prodigal children returning home, and families once marred with brokenness being healed. Congregations once divided by differing opinions began reaching out to one another to respond to the needs of the community. I witnessed prayer being offered on the streets, at newsstands, in restaurants and in businesses. These circumstances evidenced the LORD's righteousness raining down from heaven, and salvation is springing forth from the earth.[98]

I attended a week-long medical and dental clinic to serve the poorest of the poor. In the area we served, profound poverty and oppression were the way of life for thousands and had been that way for hundreds of years. When we arrived, we worked with local physicians and dentists who had finished building the walls of a medical clinic. During the week, over 8,000 people were treated, and over 3,200 individuals freely embraced the grace of God offered through faith in Jesus Christ and numerous physical healings were documented.

At the clinic, I was assigned to the prayer room where individuals who desired prayer were directed. On the first day of the clinic, there was palpable spiritual oppression in the atmosphere.

The second day of the clinic was unlike the first. On the second day, there were several manifestations of demonic deliverances in women who came for prayer. This was the first sign that the principality over the region (divination/witchcraft) that had been keeping the webs of oppression and poverty alive was now being penetrated and destroyed. On the third day, the oppressive spiritual climate had lifted, and we witnessed a record number of people spontaneously celebrating,

---

98. Isaiah 45:8

singing and dancing with joy having been told of the magnificent love of God that was offered through His beloved Son, Jesus Christ. Tears of overwhelming joy in the eyes of the people flowed unrestrained.

Because the web of lies sown over the people had been pierced, a spiritual awakening began. Individuals who had been treated at the clinic returned to their congregations to share their testimonies of faith. As a result, the local religious leaders came to the clinic for prayer.

When the leaders arrived with their Bibles in hand, the Scriptures were opened, and the Holy Spirit caused the Scriptures to "come alive" to the religious leaders. Joy filled their hears. Although these individuals arrived heavy hearted, they left filled with joy and gladness. They were also royally treated by the medical, dental and eye physicians.

The days that followed noted a record number of individuals receiving physical healings. This area of the city once darkened and oppressed by webs of witchcraft was now awakened by the flow of God's mercy and grace.

On one occasion, my interpreter asked me to pray for an eight-year-old boy born deaf and mute, brought into the prayer room by his mother. I put my hands on the ears and mouth of this precious young boy, prayed, and immediately his ears were opened, and his tongue was loosed. This young boy could now hear and speak!

The first word spoken from his mouth was "Amen" because it was the first word, he heard me speak. The boy's face lit up and tears welled up in his eyes when he heard himself speak. This miracle was told by his mother throughout the clinic and provoked a chain reaction of faith that caused other physical healings to begin to take place.

During the trip, I was often unable to sleep and often awoke at 2:00 a.m. Each morning, we met at 5:00 a.m. on the top floor of the hotel to begin the day with prayer.

One early morning, I went to the top floor and began praying in the Spirit, low enough so not to awake any guests. After about 30 minutes in prayer, I heard the door open, and an Indian man walked into the room. I stopped praying and greeted him. He said, "I was on the *first* floor of the hotel and could not sleep because I kept hearing an angelic sound coming from somewhere in the hotel, and I had to find out where it was coming from. I kept listening to the sound and found my way up to the *eleventh* floor to find it was coming from this room. What are you speaking?" he asked me.

As I stood in amazement, I opened the Scriptures to this man, visiting for one night on his way back to India. This man joyfully embraced the message of grace and mercy offered from the Lord Jesus Christ in the early hours of the morning because God made him hear an *angelic sound* coming from prayer taking place ten floors above him.

Later in the trip, our group attended a church service. At the time the offering was being received, the LORD directed me to give an offering (as well as the offering entrusted to me by a friend). At the close of the service, as the speaker was about to walk off the platform, he unexpectedly turned around and came back to the microphone and said, "I want every business owner who needs prayer to come forward. I believe God is going to cause your business to thrive and make a distinction between your business and other businesses, like God did with the children of Israel in the land of Goshen." When the speaker spoke those words, I got out of my seat and went forward for prayer. As I returned to my seat, the LORD spoke His Counsel (paraphrased):

> "You asked Me how, as the seed of Abraham, you were going to bless the nations. This is one way. When you sowed your offering in faith today, I caused the Holy Spirit to move on the pastor's heart to call business owners forward in order to release a blessing over their lives in order to make a distinction between their businesses and other businesses. It was *your* offering in

faith that caused the move of *My Spirit* to bless the business owners of this city."

Consider the Counsel of God and the unlimited and far-impacting power of an offering sown in faith after fasting and prayer.

When I returned home, I shared with my friend what the LORD had spoken regarding the offering. Her business has indeed been marked for distinction and blessing. It has received and continues to receive unsolicited promotions on Internet sites and radio and television stations.

In another account, an individual I met had been faithfully serving the LORD since her conversion six years prior; however, only after doing the Isaiah 58 fast was, she healed from emotional wounds that had come through childhood abuses. Since she was five years old, she was raised to be a lesbian. She spoke of many sexual and emotional abuses that had caused confusion about her identity as a woman and confusion about God's love toward her. During the fast, God revealed why she suffered from instability, impulsive behaviors, addictions and the inability to receive the love of God.

During her fast, the Holy Spirit broke through lies and falsehoods that had been weaved over her life through false words spoken by various mentors in her life. As a result, I watched this woman's life transform in a matter of months. She has blossomed and radiates light and life. She has begun to understand the love of God which has caused spiritual gifts she never knew she possessed to thrive.

On one occasion, this individual attended a local outing with me. The previous night she had a dream about a man walking in a field, wearing a white t-shirt and blue cap, and carrying a little black-and-white dog. On our way to the outing, we drove down a street and she pointed out the window at a man on the sidewalk and said, "That dog and that man were in my dream last night."

I turned the car around, parked and approached the man. When we approached him and the man with him, I explained to both men that the LORD had given my friend a dream about one of the men and his dog and that the LORD wanted him to know how much God loved him. As soon as the words left my lips, the Holy Spirit moved in the heart of the man with conviction, and he began to weep.

The man and his friend were from Cuba. His friend was a follower of Jesus Christ and told us he had been praying for this man and speaking to him about the LORD for many years. However, it was on this day, at this hour and at this moment, halfway around the world that God determined to open this man's spiritual eyes and bring this encounter to pass through a dream during an Isaiah 58 fast.

These amazing God stories are only a capsule of the wonderful works of God experienced as a direct result of fasting and prayer.

During your fast, I encourage you to ask the LORD to bring you a "fast partner," an individual who will fast and pray with you, someone you can account to during your fast. Pray with this person decreeing the promises of God found in Isaiah 58 while you seek the LORD to reveal any barrier or hindrance to the fulfillment of His good plans in your life. On the authority of the Word of God, when you call, He will answer you, and when you cry, He will say, "Here I am."[99]

FASTING: THE DIVINE RETURN

One morning in prayer the LORD said to me, "Every time you fast you are returning to Me." When the LORD said these words, I saw a door that was closed and a child knocking on the door. The door was the door to the Father's house. When you fast God's way, humbling

---

99. Isaiah 58:9

yourself, you become like a child, a child seeking to return to the Father in a deeper way, a child seeking to know and understand the Father's mind and heart in a deeper dimension. The Scripture states,

> At that time the disciples came to Jesus, saying, "Who then is greatest in the kingdom of heaven?"
>
> Then Jesus called a little child to Him, set him in the midst of them, and said:
>
> "Assuredly, I say to you, unless you are converted and become as little children, you will by no means enter the kingdom of heaven.
>
> Therefore whoever humbles himself as this little child is the greatest in the kingdom of heaven."
>
> —MATTHEW 18:1-4

The word "humble" in this verse is the Greek word *tapeinoo,* which means to make low or to lower oneself to a place of no importance, devoid of all arrogance and self-exaltation. Fasting is a key ingredient for obtaining humility.

The prophet Zechariah called the post-exilic house of Judah to repentance. He and the prophet Haggai were called by God to awaken the nation from its spiritual apathy. Both prophets issued a call of repentance, a call to return to the LORD. The first chapter of the book of Zechariah begins with the following words:

> In the eighth month of the second year of Darius, the word of the LORD came to Zechariah the son of Berechiah, the son of Iddo the prophet, saying,
>
> "The LORD has been very angry with your fathers.

Therefore say to them, 'Thus says the LORD of hosts: "Return to Me," says the LORD of Hosts, "and I will return to you," says the LORD of hosts.

"Do not be like your fathers, to whom the former prophets preached saying, 'Thus says the LORD of hosts: "Turn now from your evil ways and your evil deeds."' But they did not hear nor heed Me," says the LORD.

—ZECHARIAH 1:1-4

God called the nation to return to Him: "Return to Me, then I will return to you." The Hebrew word for "return" is the word *shuwb,* which means to turn back, to return, to restore, to go back and to do again. This word is a verb that describes an action by man toward reconciliation with God. The prophet admonishes the people, "Don't be like your fathers" (i.e., don't be stubborn and stiff necked), but hear the word of the LORD and turn now from your evil ways and evil deeds.

Before exile had come to Israel, the prophet Hosea prophesized this same message to the northern kingdom of Israel. At the time of Hosea's ministry, the northern kingdom appeared to have peace, plenty and prosperity, yet anarchy and rebellion lurked hidden in the heart of the nation and would ultimately bring about its collapse. The social conditions in Hosea's day included those experienced by most nations of the earth today: corrupt leaders, unstable families, prevalent immorality, class structures and poverty. The nation had a form of worship and religion, but the people failed to walk in righteousness before the LORD. In issuing a call to repentance, Hosea beckons the nation to return to the LORD and pursue the knowledge of God:

Come, and let us return to the LORD; For He has torn, but He will heal us;

He has stricken, but He will bind us up. After two days He will revive us;

On the third day he will raise us up, that we may live in His sight.

Let us know, let us pursue the knowledge of the LORD. His going forth is established as the morning; He will come to us like the rain, like the former rain to the earth.

—HOSEA 6:1-3

Fasting is God's answer for a divine return so you can pursue the knowledge of God. Although we have been torn, God is ready, willing and able to heal us and bring His restorative and refreshing rain. By returning to the LORD and applying the principles expressed in an Isaiah 58 fast, we can begin to recover the LORD's presence. It is the LORD's presence that brings "times of refreshing." It is in this place of recovery that the exceedingly great and precious promises of God are found.

Rebellion, divination and witchcraft keep you from the exceedingly great and precious promises of God. Rebellion to God appears pleasurable and justified for a moment, but the end is captivity and destruction. God said to the prophet Jeremiah that there were two evils committed by His people: they had left God and had sought to make their own cisterns to hold water but what they had made, would not hold water.

They have forsaken Me, the fountain of living waters, and hewn themselves cisterns—broken cisterns that can hold no water.

—JEREMIAH 2:13

When you rebel against God, you forsake the only source of life. Departing from God can be likened to slowing cutting off your oxygen supply. Before you know it, you are labored in your breathing and ultimately end up with no breath at all.

One of my favorite books in the Bible is the Old Testament book of Jonah. The prophet Jonah was called by God to preach repentance to the great Assyrian city of Nineveh. But this prophet did not preach repentance until God faced him with his own heart of rebellion.

Angry that God would call him to seek the repentance of a people group who committed many atrocities against the Jews, Jonah sought to "flee from the presence of the LORD."[100] He jumped onto a ship sailing to Tarshish, and the LORD sent a mighty tempest so that the mariners on the ship knew that the storm could have come only from an angry God. Jonah told the mariners that the only way for the storm to be calmed was to throw him into the sea. The mariners did as they were instructed, and the sea stopped raging. God then sent a large fish to swallow Jonah. For three days and three nights, Jonah sat in the belly of the fish, in what Jonah called "the belly of Sheol" (the inner part of the earth, the grave) away from God's presence.

Those who regard worthless idols forsake their own Mercy.

—JONAH 2:8

Jonah declared the truth about regarding (*shamar* in Hebrew meaning to keep, to preserve, to protect, observe or maintain) any idol in your life. When you observe or maintain an idol in your life, you forsake (*azab* in Hebrew meaning to leave, abandon, loose) your own mercy, the mercy of God intended to bring into your life to produce

100. Jonah 1:2

restoration. The idols in Jonah's life were pride, self-justification and unrighteous anger. These idols produced a heart of rebellion to God, rebellion to God's voice and rebellion to God's calling in Jonah's life. Jonah could not fathom how a holy and righteous God could desire to bring salvation to an unrighteous and unholy group of people. Yet, Jonah knew the character and nature of God, that God was merciful, longsuffering and always ready and willing to forgive any repentant person:

> For I know that you are gracious and merciful, slow to anger and abundant in lovingkindness, One who relents from doing harm.
>
> —JONAH 4:2

In this verse, Jonah testified to a profound spiritual truth—a truth many people do not understand. If any person continues in rebellion to God through keeping any idol in their heart, including pride, self-justification and unrighteous anger, that person will forsake the mercy of God. God's intended restoration will be halted and stayed.

If this person is you, please do not forsake the mercy of God through holding onto a worthless and vain idol. Forsaking the mercy of God is a wrong choice and not the Counsel of God for your life. Do whatever you have to do to let go of any worthless and vain idol keeping you from the mercy of God. Let go of pride, let go of anger, let go of hurt, let go of unforgiveness, let go of the offense and let go of the offender. Let go and choose the way of the LORD. Use the Isaiah 58 fast as an opportunity for God to show you every worthless, vain and damaging idol that has been erected in your life. Use the Isaiah 58 fast to acknowledge that you don't have to be right or self-justified anymore; you can be wrong and being wrong before the LORD is OK.

Use the Isaiah 58 fast to forgive the individual(s) who hurt you or the one who owes you an apology. Let go of the anger you may have developed at God's love toward your enemies. Let go of any pride that may be keeping you from developing true Christ-like humility. Once you let go of the idols, you will be able to freely enjoy the everlasting mercies of God and the river of His divine grace flowing in and to you. Restoration is the LORD's inheritance waiting for you and the sure and certain Counsel of God for you.

PRAYER

Father, I come before You and ask You to search my heart. Search me and find any place of rebellion residing in my life. I ask You to put my heart on trial. Find me out. Uncover and burn away all iniquity and sin in my life. Reveal any unrighteous yokes, alliances and agreements I have made with any individual or organization that has caused me to have a divided heart toward You.

Reveal any covenants of death I made with my mouth or my heart. Reveal sins committed throughout my generations where we have agreed with rebellion or have aligned our lives with others in rebellion to You. I repent of all agreements and covenants I made with my mouth and with my heart when I was in defiance and in rebellion toward You.

I renounce, reject and disclaim any agreements made with drugs, alcohol, pornography, sexual sins, immorality, greed, envy and covetousness. I renounce, reject and disclaim any agreements made with individuals who are or were in rebellion to You. I renounce, reject and disclaim any oath or pledge I made to anyone other than You or to my spouse made in our covenant marriage vows.

I renounce, reject and disclaim any agreements made with witches, warlocks, palm-readers, sorcerers, diviners, horoscopes, shaman, spiritualists and spirit guides. I renounce reject and disclaim any agreements made with false prophesies and false words decreed or spoken over my life and the life of my family.

I was created by You, in You, through You and for You. I choose Your words of life, Your words of peace and Your words of hope. I ask You to forgive me and cleanse me for looking to anything other than You for my direction, guidance and healing. Forgive me for making unrighteous agreements with my mouth and with my heart. I repent of my rebellion to You and Your Law.

I acknowledge that You are all light and life, and I choose to walk in Your light and life. I choose to return to You with all my heart. I choose Your Word for my counsel, direction and guidance in my life and my future. Amen.

CHAPTER FIVE

NEVER, NEVER, NEVER GIVE UP

uring World War II, when facing a formidable enemy with no sign of victory in sight, Winston Churchill delivered these words to the graduating class at Harrow School:

> "Never give in—never, never, never—in nothing great or small, large or petty, never give in except to convictions of honour and good sense. Never yield to force; never yield to the apparently overwhelming might of the enemy."[101]

Don't ever give up pursuing restoration. No matter how much damage the enemy has rendered, restoration in God's eyes is so much

---

101. "The Unrelenting Struggle" delivered by Winston Churchill at Harrow School in October 1941

more than any damage or destruction the enemy has accomplished. The Scripture promises:

> Eye has not seen, nor ear heard, nor have entered into the heart of man the things which God has prepared for those who love him.
>
> —1 CORINTHIANS 2:9

King David and the Apostle Paul are perfect examples of pursuing the Counsel of God and accomplishing restoration for their lives and the lives of future generations.

King David and the nation of Israel's recovery did not end when David took possession of Jerusalem.[102] Although King David had moved into the stronghold (aka the City of David), he had not yet taken possession of the Mt. Moriah, which at that time was in the hands of the Jebusites. Mt. Moriah is the location where Abraham confirmed his faith in God by offering his promised son Isaac as an offering to God. The Scripture declares,

> Now it came to pass after these things that God tested Abraham, and said to him, "Abraham!" And he said, "Here I am." Then He said, "Take now your son, your only son Isaac, whom you love, and go to the land of Moriah, and offer him there as a burnt offering on one of the mountains of which I shall tell you."
>
> —GENESIS 22:1-2

Mt. Moriah is also the location where God told King Solomon to build the temple.[103] King David and the nation of Israel came into

---

102. 2 Samuel 5

103. 2 Chronicles 3:1

possession of Mt. Moriah quite differently from any other land acquisition. Previously, King David obtained possession of cities and land by going to battle. This time however, possession of Mt. Moriah did not come through war, but through an eternal covenant of mercy, the covenant God had previously made with King David and his seed:

> When your days are fulfilled and you rest with your fathers, I will set up your seed after you, who will come from your body, and I will establish his kingdom.
>
> He shall build a house for My name, and I will establish the throne of his kingdom forever.
>
> I will be his Father, and he shall be My son. If he commits iniquity, I will chasten him with the rod of men and with the blows of the sons of men.
>
> But My mercy shall not depart from him, as I took it from Saul, whom I removed from before you.
>
> And your house and your kingdom shall be established forever before you. Your throne shall be established forever.
>
> —2 SAMUEL 7:12-16

Second Samuel 24 instructs that the possession of Mt. Moriah came after David ordered a census of his army. The Scripture also states that it was the "anger of the LORD" aroused against Israel that caused David to "Go, number Israel and Judah."[104]

After the census was ordered, the Scripture states that "David's heart condemned him," and he repented.[105] Upon his repentance, the LORD

---

104. 2 Samuel 24:1

105. 2 Samuel 24:10

sent the prophet Gad to King David to allow him to choose one of three judgments the LORD offered for his sin:

> So Gad came to David and told him; and said to him, "Shall seven years of famine come to you in your land? Or shall you flee three months before your enemies, while they pursue you? Or shall there be three days' plague in your land? Now consider and see what answer I should take back to Him who sent me."
>
> And David said to Gad, "I am in great distress. Please let us fall into the hand of the LORD for His mercies are great; but do not let me fall into the hand of man."
>
> So the Lord sent a plague upon Israel from the morning till the appointed time. From Dan to Beersheba seventy thousand men of the people died.
>
> And when the angel stretched out His hand over Jerusalem to destroy it, the Lord relented from the destruction, and said to the angel who was destroying the people, "It is enough; now restrain your hand." And the angel of the Lord was by the threshing floor of Araunah the Jebusite.
>
> —2 SAMUEL 24:13-16

King David had sinned in ordering the census. The LORD is righteous and therefore must punish sin but, in this instance, allowed King David to choose his punishment. King David chose three days of plague in the land, the method he believed would put him in the hands of God's mercy. As a result of the plague, 70,000 men of Israel died. After the plague, an angel of the LORD came into Jerusalem to destroy it, but the LORD stopped the angel.[106]

---

106. 2 Samuel 24:16

Because God had previously made a covenant of mercy with David, the LORD cut short the intended judgment. God then commanded the administrator of His judgment, the angel of the LORD, to cease from destroying Jerusalem and to stand watch at the threshing floor of Araunah the Jebusite. In the meantime, the LORD instructed the prophet Gad to tell King David that he needed to erect an altar on the threshing floor of Araunah the Jebusite.[107]

Stewardship of Mt. Moriah lay in the hands of Araunah the Jebusite. However, Mt. Moriah was in the hands of Araunah the Jebusite only until God was ready turn the possession of it over to King David and the nation of Israel. Hear this truth: It was through King David's sin that God gave King David and the nation an opportunity to possess their inheritance.

Then Araunah, said, "Why has my lord the king come to his servant?"

And David said, "To buy the threshing floor from you, to build an altar to the LORD, that the plague may be withdrawn from the people."

Now Araunah said to David, "Let my lord the king take and offer up whatever seems good to him. Look, here are oxen from burnt sacrifice, and threshing implements and the yokes of the oxen for wood.

All these, O king, Araunah has given to the king."

And Araunah said to the king, "May the LORD your God accept you."

Then the king said to Araunah, "No, but I will surely buy it from you for a price; nor will I offer burnt offerings to the LORD my God with that which costs me nothing." So David bought the threshing floor and the oxen for fifty shekels of silver.

---

107. 2 Samuel 24:18

And David built there an altar to the LORD, and offered burnt offerings and peace offerings. So the LORD heeded the prayers for the land, and the plague was withdrawn from Israel.

—2 SAMUEL 24:21-25

Knowing that the nation and it's king would both commit sin and later seek repentance leading to restoration, God reserved for the nation and King David a place to bestow His covenant mercy and a place to receive an offering of atonement.

Why was King David required to purchase the threshing floor of Araunah? Because the threshing floor was the location where Abraham's faith in God was confirmed through a faith sacrifice. Abraham called the name of the place of sacrifice, "The LORD Will Provide" (or in Hebrew, *YHWH Yireh)*, as it is said to this day, "In the Mount of the LORD, it shall be provided."[108]

King David knew he had sinned and that his sin had cost 70,000 innocent lives. To atone for the sin, the prophet Gad tells King David to erect an altar to the LORD on the threshing floor of Arunah, and he did according to the word of Gad (2 Samuel 24:18). When King David approached Araunah to request the purchase of the threshing floor to stop the plague, Arunah was willing to give King David not only the threshing floor, but also the oxen needed for sacrifice. King David, not willing to take that which cost him nothing, declared,

"No, but I will surely buy it from you for a price: nor will I offer burnt offerings to the LORD my God with that which costs me nothing."

—2 SAMUEL 24:24

---

108. Genesis 22:14

King David built an altar to the LORD and offered burnt offerings and peace offerings (2 Samuel 24:5). The LORD heeded the prayers and offering of King David, and the plague was withdrawn from Israel.

The LORD foreknew and prepared every type of provision needed for faith to be confirmed. To Abraham, the LORD brought a ram for a sacrifice. In the same location, the LORD provided King David with provision for the purchase of the threshing floor and the oxen needed for the sacrifice.

LIKE ABRAHAM AND KING DAVID, GOD HAS PREPARED DIVINE PROVISION FOR YOUR RESTORATION

Like King David's life attests, even if you have sinned, have dropped the ball or failed to fulfill the Counsel of the LORD up to this day, there is great news for you—God foreknew your sin and has gone before you to provide provision to make atonement and a covering for every failure, every sin. The Scripture declares,

> In Him we have obtained an inheritance, being predestined according to the purpose of Him who works all things according to the counsel of His will, that we who first trusted in Christ should be to the praise of His glory.
>
> —EPHESIANS 1:11

The Greek word for "predestined" is the word *proorizo,* which means to determine or decide beforehand and is used to declare God's eternal decrees and plan of salvation, its benefits, and our adoption and inheritance as sons and daughters. Just as the LORD worked out His eternal and predestined will hidden amid King David's sin, God is working out His divine will amid our past sins and in our present circumstances.

One day, when I was thinking about past sin, the LORD spoke to me about how He had used the sin in King David's life to fulfill His divine purposes. The LORD then spoke these encouraging words, "You are my covenant child, there is no sin that you commit that I have not already known and have not already gone before you to make provision for—not only to cover the sin, but to perform My eternal Counsel in your life."

God's Counsel in your life can be performed no matter what past sin has been committed. His covenant of mercy and grace is far, far greater than any sin.

GOD'S COUNSEL ALWAYS PREVAILS

Like King David, the Apostle Paul fulfilled the Counsel of the Lord. Even though Paul had untold numbers of enemies in his life—enemies plotting, scheming, strategizing and decreeing destruction over him—the Counsel of the LORD always prevailed. Men in Jerusalem continually plotted to kill him.[109] He was stoned and left for dead.[110] By oath of death over forty men plotted to kill him.[111] A tempest wind blew a storm intended for his death while he was at sea,[112] and a deadly snake bit him.[113]

---

109. Acts 9:23,29

110. Acts 14:19

111. Acts 23:12-14

112. Acts 27: 13-38

113. Acts 28:3-6

Nevertheless, Paul had a mandate from God to go from Jerusalem to Rome.[114] Once he was rejected by the Jews in Jerusalem, the gospel message could be delivered to the Gentile world.[115] This blessing for the Gentile world was the foredetermined Counsel of the LORD that could not be nullified or cancelled, no matter what formidable opponents were arrayed against God's messenger of truth.

Once Paul arrived in Rome, for the first time in his ministry, he was free to preach the gospel with all confidence with no one forbidding him.[116] If Paul had given up during his arduous journey between Jerusalem and Rome, he would never have fulfilled his life purpose which was to preach the gospel of grace to the Gentile world. The Apostle Paul never surrendered to adverse circumstances in his race of faith and neither should you. Keep running and don't stop running—the LORD is with you.

I want to encourage you with a 21st Century testimony of faith. A minister was conducting a weeklong healing crusade. Each night of the crusade, a child brought her blind mother to the platform to be given sight. Each night the minister prayed for the blind woman. Although the woman was touched by the Holy Spirit, each night she left blind.

On the last night of the crusade, the minister thought to himself, "I am not going to pray for this lady for nothing has happened each time I have prayed," and he turned to walk away. After he turned away, the Holy Spirit said to him, "Go back and pray for that woman." The minister thought, "I have prayed for her each night of the crusade and nothing has happened," but he heeded the voice of the LORD. As the

---

114. Acts 19:21, 27:24

115. Acts 28:25-28

116. Acts 28:31

minister laid his hands on the blind woman, her eyes opened. The minister was amazed.

A few weeks later, the Holy Spirit recalled the woman at the crusade and showed the minister a vision of the woman. In the vision, the woman had an octopus-like figure on her head. After each evening of prayer, one of the tentacles or arms of the octopus was removed. By the last evening, the entire octopus-looking figure was removed, and she could receive her healing. Had the minister or the woman stopped short of the last night of prayer, the woman would not have received her healing.

After I heard this testimony, my faith soared, and my perseverance increased. This story is an excellent example of the result of partnering with God in perseverance until all spiritual tentacles in your life are removed. Do not stop short of your full restoration. Stay in the race. Keep the faith.

Ask the LORD, "What are the 'tentacles' in my life that need to be removed?" Then, ask the LORD to show you what may be holding back your restoration.

It is by faith that the promises of God are obtained[117], and it is by faith that we overcome the world.[118] It takes faith to fast, it takes faith to pray, and it takes faith to persevere when you have been persevering and don't yet see the manifestation of your promise. God is faithful and true to His Word. He cannot lie, and His Word cannot return void, so "Never, Never, Never give up!"

---

117. Galatians 3:14, Romans 4:20

118. 1 John 5:4

MORE THAN CONQUERORS

I want to share with you a battle that has for years motivated and inspired me. The Battle of San Jacinto fought on April 21, 1836 in present day Harris County, Texas. In this decisive battle, Texas gained its independence from a vicious and oppressive dictator, Antonio Lopez de Santa Anna.

However, before victory came at San Jacinto, in a miraculous 18 minutes, the men of Texas had suffered two bloody and costly defeats: The Goliad Campaign and The Battle of the Alamo. Had the men not continued to fight and forge forward rallying cries of "Remember the Alamo!" and "Remember Goliad!" although they had previously witnessed only defeat, they would never have experienced a most decisive and miraculous victory. If these brave men had stopped short of the battle at San Jacinto, they would not have witnessed the miracle provision of victory for their families and for future of generations yet to come.

Romans 8:37 declares that in all things we are *more than conquerors* through Christ who loves us. The Greek word for the phrase "more than conquerors" used in this context is *hupernikao* and means one who is super-victorious, a person who wins more than an ordinary victory. In fact, it means someone who wins an abundant victory. This is you! God has purposed an abundant, more than ordinary victory for you!

Make a decisive decision today to never stop pursing restoration. Decide today to run your race of faith in partnership with the LORD. Ask the LORD to reveal any tentacle that has bound you or has hindered your victorious race of faith. Be assured, the LORD has already provided the provision necessary for you to experience total victory.

Decide today to return to your first love, Jesus Christ. Not only will the present generations have you to thank, but future generations as well. Remember, never, never, never give up. You have come too far. Your blood, sweat and tears are much too valuable to the LORD.

Consider these encouraging words from Theodore Roosevelt, the 26th President of the United States:

> It's not the critic who counts; not the man who points out how the strong man stumbles, or where the doer of deeds could have done them better. The credit belongs to the man who is actually in the arena, who face if marred by dust and sweat and blood; who strives valiantly; who errs, who comes short again and again, because there is no effort without error and shortcoming; but he who does actually strive to do the deeds.

YOUR AIM: TO KNOW GOD

While preparing for an Isaiah 58 fast, the LORD said, "My people do not really *know* Me." The LORD was not speaking in the sense of not having salvation in Him, but rather from a relational standpoint of His people not truly knowing Him, His character, His nature, His DNA. You can have eternal life by grace through faith in Jesus Christ and have the divine nature of God is living inside of you, but this is not the same as *knowing* God.

I can be born into a family, carry the family name, have the physical likeness of my father, and even receive an inheritance when my father dies without ever knowing my father. If I don't know my father, then I will simply take what he has given me as a matter of birthright; however, I will never obtain the privilege and honor of knowing him personally and knowing his heart toward me. Without knowing my father, his endowments and gifts have less value and meaning. Without knowing my father, I may carry his name, but I will never be truly like him in heart and mind.

On the other hand, if I know my father and know his heart toward me, then when he gives me a word of encouragement, a loving stoke, or word of instruction, I am eager, willing and diligent to receive and obey him by virtue of knowing him and understanding his love for me. Because I know him, I know his heart toward me, which makes me love and trust him even more.

In like manner, the LORD wants His children to *know* Him personally and intimately. When you know the LORD intimately, you can love Him with all your heart, mind and soul, and you can receive His love toward you. When you abide in His love, you begin to know Him. In knowing Him, you become eager, willing and diligent to follow and obey Him.

The Apostle Paul had in mind the importance of pursing the knowledge of God when he penned the following two inspired prayers to Christians living in the city of Ephesus:

> Therefore I also, after I heard of your faith in the LORD Jesus and your love for all the saints,
>
> Do not cease to give thanks for you, making mention of you in my prayers:
>
> That the God of our Lord Jesus Christ, the Father of glory, may give to you the spirit of wisdom and revelation in the knowledge of Him,
>
> The eyes of your understanding being enlightened; that you may know what is the hope of His calling, what are the riches of the glory of His inheritance in the saints,
>
> And what is the exceeding greatness of His power toward us who believe, according to the working of His mighty power.
>
> —EPHESIANS 1:15-19

For this reason I bow my knees to the Father of our Lord Jesus Christ; from whom the whole family in heaven and earth is named,

That He would grant you, according to the riches of His glory, to be strengthened with might through His Spirit in the inner man,

That Christ may dwell in your hearts through faith; that you, being rooted and grounded in love,

May be able to comprehend with all the saints what is the width and length and depth and height—

To know the love of Christ which passes knowledge; that you may be filled with all the fullness of God.

—EPHESIANS 3:14-19

There are several words in the Hebrew and Greek for the word "know" or "knowledge" of God. The word for "knowledge" used in Ephesians 1:17 is the Greek word *epignosis,* which means coming into the acceptance or full knowledge of God. In these two passages, the Apostle Paul said that when you come into the knowledge of God you will:

1) know the hope of your calling in Christ,

2) know the exceeding richness of the glory of the inheritance in the saints in Christ,

3) know the greatness of God's power in Christ, and

4) know the width, length, depth and height, to know the love of Christ.

The Old Testament prophets Hosea and Jeremiah also speak about what it means to *know* God. Both prophets use a form of the Hebrew word *da'ath,* which is used in a sense of knowing by experience, relationship or encounter.

Jeremiah denounces Jehoiakim, King of Judah, for his lavish living and the building of his kingdom using forced labor, paying unjust wages and, otherwise, severely oppressing the people. In this regard, Jeremiah poses a question to the king concerning his righteous father:

> "Shall you reign because you enclose yourself in cedar? Did not your father eat and drink and do justice and righteousness? Then it was well with him.
>
> He judged the cause of the poor and needy. Then it was well.
>
> Was not this knowing ME?" says the LORD.
>
> "Yet your eyes and your heart are for nothing but your covetousness, for shedding innocent blood, and practicing oppression and violence."
>
> —JEREMIAH 22:15-17

Jeremiah declares the abominable actions of King Jehoiakim, the actions of gaining wealth through unjust means and failing to do what was just and right for the poor. The prophet questions King Jehoiakim by highlighting the wellness of his father's kingdom that came as a result of his father pursuing the knowledge of God—God's justice and righteousness—when "He judged the cause of the poor and needy." Then the LORD rhetorically asks, "Was not this *knowing* Me?"

In like manner, the prophet Hosea brings a charge of the LORD against the children of Israel for failing to have the knowledge of God in their land:

> Hear the word of the LORD, you children of Israel, for the

LORD brings a charge against the inhabitants of the land:

"There is no truth or mercy or knowledge of God in the land.

By swearing and lying, killing and stealing and committing adultery, they break all restraint, with bloodshed upon bloodshed.

Therefore the land will mourn; and everyone who dwells there will waste away with the beasts of the field and the birds of the air; even the fish of the sea will be taken away."

—HOSEA 4:1-3

As a result of not having the knowledge of God in the land, there was no truth or mercy in the hearts of the people. Because there was no truth or mercy in the heart of the people, the people broke all restraint with bloodshed upon bloodshed by lying, killing, stealing and committing adultery. As a result of these conditions, the land that was created to flourish and thrive mourned because only waste and destruction were found.

Hosea describes the same conditions outlined in Isaiah 59, conditions that existed because there was no knowledge of God in the land:

"Their webs will not become garments, nor will they cover themselves with their works;

Their works are works of iniquity, and the act of violence is in their hands.

Their feet run to evil, and they make haste to shed innocent blood;

Their thoughts are thoughts of iniquity; wasting and destruction are in their paths.

The way of peace they have not known,

And there is no justice in their ways; they have made themselves crooked paths;

Whoever takes that way shall not know peace."

—ISAIAH 59:6-8

The Apostle James describes the test of knowing God when he declares what pure, sincere and undefiled religion is "to visit orphans and widows in their trouble and to keep oneself unspotted from the world."[119]

In James 2:1-9, the Apostle outlines the sin that has kept Christians from evidencing true and pure religion: personal favoritism or holding biases and prejudices for or against poor brothers and sisters. James gives examples, one of which includes paying greater attention to the one in the congregation wearing "fine clothes" to the detriment of the person in the congregation wearing "filthy" clothes. James rebukes the brethren who have failed in their ethical duty to each other and their "poor brethren," and says,

Have you not shown partiality among yourselves and become judges with evil thoughts?

Listen, my beloved brethren: Has God not chosen the poor of this world to be rich in faith and heirs of the kingdom which he promised to those who love Him?

But you have dishonored the poor man. Do not the rich drag you into the courts?

Do they not blaspheme that noble name by which you are called?

119. James 1:27

If you really fulfill the royal law according to the Scripture, "You shall love your neighbor as yourself," you do well;

But if you show partiality, you commit sin, and are convicted by the law of transgressors.

—JAMES 2:4-9

James states that when Christians show partiality toward each other, they pervert the knowledge of God's righteousness and justice. Before we can expect the world around us to change and for others to desire the knowledge of God, Christians must pursue and live out the knowledge of God among themselves, among the brethren.

In Deuteronomy, God instructed Moses to appoint judges and officers in the gates of the city in order to judge the matters of the people with justice. When the judges evaluated a case, they were instructed as follows:

You shall not pervert justice; you shall not show partiality, nor take a bribe for a bribe blinds the eyes of the wise and twists the words of the righteous.

You shall follow what is altogether just, that you may live and inherit the land which the LORD your God is giving you.

—DEUTERONOMY 16:19-20

The Apostle James used the law of God taken from the law of Moses found in the book of Deuteronomy and puts it into practical application through the royal law of love.

James 2:4 states that when we show partiality, we become judges with evil thoughts. The word "thoughts" in this Scripture is the word *dialogismos,* which means inward reasoning, deliberation and the reckoning of man. When we show partiality, our inward reasoning, deliberation and reckoning becomes perverted or evil. As a result, we fail to judge a matter with God's righteous judgments and, therefore, commit sin.

How would you like to be judged by other Christians (not the world) with unrighteous scales and partiality? No person wants to be judged with unrighteous scales. Making righteous evaluations and judgments are one of the seminal reasons we must diligently pursue and seek the *knowledge* of God. The LORD desperately desires His children to righteously evaluate matters and have no partiality in our judgments. It is only then that true justice can be established in our hearts, our spheres of influence and in our land. When righteous judgments are issued, the web of lies over our lives and families can be destroyed.

Ask the LORD to reveal any inward reasoning, deliberation and reckoning that has produced partiality in your judgments toward others, the rich and the poor alike. Ask the LORD to purge you and cleanse you from any trace of evil reasoning and reckoning in your mind and heart concerning individuals of a different race, tribe or even Christian denomination. Ask the LORD to grant you forgiveness for perverting His scales of justice. Repent of any agreements with partiality, perversion in judgments and evil. Jealousy, envy, strife and competition with others will produce partiality and evil inward reasoning.

GOD'S SCALES ALWAYS BALANCE

God scales are only just and equitable. God's scales always balance in righteousness, there are no exceptions.[120] However, when we, as God's agents in the earth, show partiality, we pervert and distort God's scales of justice. When perversion happens, we become agents of unrighteousness. Unrighteousness is sin. You do not have to be a judge or a lawyer to be guilty of this sin. Every day each one of us

---

120. Proverbs 16:11

form judgments in our hearts and minds about others based on evil deliberations and reckonings. This kind of judgement is sin. When we form unrighteous judgments, we not only dishonor God, but we become the person who perpetuates the weaving of webs of lies, rather than the person who destroys and removes the webs of lies.

Although neither the prophets nor the apostles provide an exhaustive list of evidence of a person's knowledge of God, the Scriptures do provide many useful examples to measure our *da'at* of God. Ask yourself, how does my knowledge of God measure up according to the Word of God? Based on the words of the prophets and apostles, do I have pure and undefiled religion? Take time with the LORD to sincerely consider these questions. In doing so ask, yourself, "Does my heart, my giving and my life actions line up with the knowledge of God found in the Word of God?" If I truly know the LORD the way He intends for me to know Him, my heart, hands, feet and mouth will conform to His Word toward my brothers, sisters, neighbors, widows, orphans and especially those who are poor, helpless and suffering in this world.

Pleading and advocating for the cause of the poor and voiceless is our duty. We are all advocates, ambassadors and representatives of the LORD and His righteousness on Earth.[121] Speaking out for those who have no voice or those have lost their voice, is righteousness.[122] Seeking the wellbeing of the widow and the fatherless is true and undefiled religion and is evidence of knowing God. Simply writing a check will not satisfy God's standard of righteousness. There must be a sincere heart change toward mercy, God's mercy toward others.

Isaiah 58 and Matthew 5 and 6 declare the knowledge of God and what God is looking for among His people. As you fast according to

---

121. 2 Corinthians 5:20

122. Proverbs 31:8-9

Isaiah 58, seek the *da 'at* of God with all of your heart. God promises that when you do, He will be found by you, and He will not only turn your captivity,[123] but also, according to Isaiah 58:8, will cause your healing to spring forth speedily.

In the book of Revelation, Jesus Christ counsels His seven churches in Asia Minor. To the church in Laodicea, the LORD instructs the church to buy gold refined in the fire. The LORD states,

> "I know your works, that you are neither cold or hot. I could wish you were cold or hot.
>
> So then, because you are lukewarm, and neither cold or hot, I will vomit you out of My mouth. Because you say, I am rich, have become wealthy, and have need of nothing—and do not know that you are wretched, miserable, poor, blind and naked—
>
> I counsel you to buy from Me gold refined in the fire, that you may be rich; and white garments, that you may be clothed, that the shame of your nakedness may not be revealed; and anoint your eyes with eye salve, that you may see."
>
> —REVELATION 3:15-21

In evaluating the church in Laodicea, the LORD said they were blind to their own nakedness. In other words, they had no eternal works of righteousness to cover themselves; therefore, they stood naked before God. Their nakedness consisted of dead works that amounted to nothing before the LORD. These are not works of righteousness for salvation, but rather works of righteousness because of their salvation. Because the church was lukewarm in heart, the garments of their righteous works were lacking.

---

123. Jeremiah 29:13-14

Jesus Christ counsels His church to go and buy gold refined in the fire. He tells them to go and find out what true works of righteousness consist of and do them. He tells them they are clothed in shame because they profess faith in Him but have no works of righteousness to support their profession of faith. Their clothing was not rich and white, symbolizing works of true and sincere righteousness, but rather they were shamefully naked.

God anointed Jesus Christ with the Holy Spirit and with power, and He went about doing good and healing all who were oppressed by the devil.[124] As an imitator of God, we are all to be about doing good, not from the head but from the heart. Don't misunderstand. God is not interested in our "works" for Him, but He is interested in our heart toward Him. When our heart has embraced the knowledge of God, our hands will go about doing good and our works will be found clean and righteous.

In James 2:17-22, the Apostle states that without works to support your profession of faith you have a dead religion, yet faith along with works causes your faith to be made perfect.

The word "perfect" in James 2:22 is the word *teleioo,* and means to complete, accomplish, carry through to the end and bring to a successful conclusion or maturity. Faith in Jesus Christ is brought to maturity by works of righteousness. If you are not doing works of righteousness in your daily living 1) you do not truly *know* God the way He wants you to *know* Him, and 2) your faith has not matured. It is only through works of righteousness that we come to *know* God and mature in faith.

Pursue the *knowledge* of God. Consider your life now and ask yourself, "Do I really *know* God? Will I be ashamed at the LORD's coming? Will I be able stand unashamed before the LORD? Will I be clothed

---

124. Acts 10:38

in white garments showing a true and sincere faith that is evidenced by works of true righteousness or will my garments be soiled, or worse, will I be standing naked?"

Take time to evaluate your works now. Ask God to show you where you need to make corrections and make them. Sincerely find out where your garments may be soiled and shameful. The LORD instructs us to do this.[125] God wants us to evaluate our works before Him now so we can make any needed corrections.

The Apostle John instructs of a divine test to determine if we truly know God. That test hinges on whether we keep the commandments of God:

> Now by this we know that we know Him, if we keep His commandments.
>
> He who says, "I know Him," and does not keep His commandments, is a lair, and the truth is not in him.
>
> But whoever keeps His word, truly the love of God is perfected in him. By this we know that we are in Him.
>
> —1 JOHN 2:3-5

Based on this Scripture, the test to determine if we know God and are found in Him is: Do we keep His commandments? If anyone says that he knows God and does not keep the LORD's command to love, that person is a liar and the truth is not in him.

> Therefore we also, since we are surrounded by so great a cloud of witnesses, let us lay aside every weight and the sin that so easily

---

125. Revelation 3:18

ensnares us, and let us run with endurance the race that is set before us,

Looking unto Jesus, the author and finisher of our faith, who for the joy that was set before Him endured the cross, despising the shame and has sat down at the right hand of the throne of God.

—HEBREWS 12:1-2

Is anything keeping you for pursing the knowledge of God from your heart? If so, lay aside every weight that has kept you from pursing the knowledge of the LORD. Pursing the knowledge of God from your heart and with all your heart. Know God. Know Him. In Him is you present and in Him is your future. In Him is found your *Divine Restoration.*

ℋow to Fulfill the Greatest Commandment of God

$\mathcal{M}$oses was summoned by God to lead the nation of Israel out of Egypt into the land of Canaan, the territory promised by God to Abraham and his seed.[126] Moses shepherded the nation through the desert of Sinai toward Canaan. During this travel, God directed the nation to stop at Mt. Sinai. It was on this mountain that God revealed Himself to a people He had chosen for Himself. It was also on this mountain that God called the children of Israel a special treasure above all the people on the earth, a kingdom of priests, a holy nation.[127]

At Mt. Sinai, God summoned Moses to the top of the mountain to meet with Him face to face and to declare the Law of God.[128] God then wrote His Laws, also called the Ten Commandments, with His finger

---

126. Genesis 12:1, 17:7-8

127. Exodus 19:5-6

128. Exodus 18:20

on two tables cut out of stone.[129] The word "commandments" is the Hebrew word *mitzvah,* which means command, ordinance, precept, law or directives. Moses received the tablets of stone, came down the mountain and called the children of Israel together to hear the Law of God "that they may observe them *and* do them."[130] Moses instructed the nation to:

> Now this is the commandment, and these are the statutes and judgments which the LORD your God has commanded to teach you, that you may observe them in the land which you are crossing over to possess,
>
> That you may fear the LORD your God, to keep all His statutes and His commandments which I command you, you and your son and your grandson, all the days of your life, and that your days may be prolonged.
>
> Therefore hear, O Israel, and be careful to observe it, that it may be well with you that you may multiply greatly as the LORD God of your fathers has promised you—"a land flowing with milk and honey."
>
> Hear, O Israel: The LORD our God, the LORD is one!
>
> You shall love the LORD your God with all your heart, with all your soul, and with all your strength.
>
> And these word which I command you today shall be in your heart.
>
> You shall teach them diligently to your children, and shall talk of them when you sit in your house, when you walk by the way, when you lie down and when you rise up.

---

129. Exodus 24:12, 31:18

130. Deuteronomy 5:1

You shall write them as a sign on your hand, and they shall be as frontlets between your eyes.

You shall write them on the doorposts of your house and on your gates.

—DEUTERONOMY 6:1-9

Although God commanded obedience to His laws, the nation's obedience was to arise from a relationship based on love. The word "love" used in Deuteronomy 6 is the word *ahab,* which is to love like a friend or to have affection for. The word for *heart* in this Scripture is the word *leb,* which is the inner self, the inner yearnings, the intellect, mind and deepest feelings of self. For the nation to fulfill the commandments of God, the individuals comprising the nation would have to learn to love the LORD with all their heart, intellect, inner yearnings and deepest feelings.

Jesus Christ quoted these passages from Deuteronomy when addressing the greatest commandment of God.[131] In Matthew 22, Christ is asked by a lawyer and Pharisee, one of Israel's teachers of the law of Moses, which of the commandments of God was the greatest. Jesus responds to him by quoting Deuteronomy 6:5 and saying,

"'You shall love the Lord your God with all your heart, with all your soul, and with all your mind.' This is *the* first and great commandment. And *the* second *is* like it: 'You shall love your neighbor as yourself.'

—MATTHEW 22:37-40

---

131. Mark 12:30, Luke 10:27, Matthew 22:37

In His response, Christ summed up in one word the moral obligations in the law of God, the moral obligations of man toward God and man toward man: Love. However, Christ used the word *agapao* for the word *love* when He quoted Deuteronomy 6:5, not the word *ahab*. The word *agapao* is the word for unconditional love. It is love by choice and by an act of the will. *Agapao* is love that will seek the highest good of another. This is not the word for *love* used in Deuteronomy 6:5 when Moses says, "You shall *love* (*ahab*) the LORD with all your heart and soul." *Ahab* love is not the highest form of love. Rather, the highest form of love is *agapao* love, used only in the New Testament when Jesus Christ declared the greatest commandment of God.[132]

God gave the world *agapao* love when God gave His Son, Jesus Christ, as the sole and perfect sacrifice for every transgression, every iniquity and every sin committed by man. John 3:16 declares:

> For God so *loved* (*agapao*) the world that He gave His only begotten Son, that whoever believes in Him should not perish but have everlasting life.

The Apostle John also uses the word *agapao* when he writes that we are "to *love* one another, for *love* is from God and everyone who *loves* is born of God and knows God. But the one who does not *love* does not know God, for God is *love*."[133]

One day, the Holy Spirit said to me, "The reason My people do not fulfill the greatest commandment is because they have lust mixed up with love." As I considered this statement, I contemplated the multitude of forces in the universe composed of lust that compete with the pure *agapao* love of God.

---

132. Matthew 22:37-40

133. 1 John 4:7-8

We are commanded to pursue agape love.[134] We are to seek to develop this virtue because it is not a virtue we naturally possess. Rather, it is of divine origin. The Scripture states that if we love the world and the things of the world, the love of God is not in us:

> Do not love the world or the things in the world. If anyone loves the world, the love of the Father is not in him.
>
> For all that is in the world—the lust of the flesh, the lust of the eye, and the pride of life—is not of the Father, but is of the world.
>
> And the world is passing away, and the lust of it; but he who does the will of God abides forever.
>
> —1 JOHN 2:15-17

The Apostle John states that all that is in the world and appeals to the senses is lust. The word "lust" used in 1 John 2" is the Greek word *epithumia,* which means a strong desire and intense craving for something, including gratifying sensual cravings, coveting what belongs to another, and even consists of striving for things, persons or experiences contrary to the will of God.

We cannot fulfill the greatest commandment of God on which hang all the prophets and the law, the command to *agapao* God with all our heart and *agapao* our neighbor as ourselves when we love the world and the things of the world. It is impossible. It cannot be done. There is an inherent conflict of interest between the interests of the world and the interests of God. Jesus Christ told us that loving the world and loving God would be impossible when He said, "No servant can serve two masters; for either he will hate the one and love the other, or else he

---

134. 1 Corinthians 14:1

will be loyal to the one and despise the other. You cannot serve God and mammon."[135]

The Scripture admonishes us to "flee also youthful lusts, but pursue, righteousness, faith, love, and peace with those who call on the Lord out of a pure heart."[136] Youthful lusts consist of strong desires, intense cravings, gratifying of sensual cravings, coveting what belongs to another or striving for things that are not the will of God. God tells us to flee from these things. Not only are we to actively and aggressively flee lusts, pursuits and strivings that are not the will of God, but we must direct our strivings and desires to actively and aggressively pursue righteousness, faith, love, and peace with other Christians.

These admonitions sound like an impossible pursuit and would be impossible if we had to do these actions using our own effort and strength. God does not ask us to obey Him in our own strength. It is impossible for us to obey the LORD and to overcome lust in our own strength. Only divine power can overcome the carnal nature and fleshly desires. God gave us His divine power when He gifted us with part of Himself, the Holy Spirit that lives inside of us. The Holy Spirit is the powerhouse within that gives us the ability and authority to have dominion and ruling power over the flesh and its lustful desires and pursuits. The Apostle Paul states in Galatians 5:16-17, 24-24,

> I say then: Walk in the Spirit, and you shall not fulfill the lust of the flesh.
>
> For the flesh lusts against the Spirit, and the Spirit against the flesh; and these are contrary to one another, so that you do not do the things that you wish.

---

135. Luke 16:13

136. 2 Timothy 2:22

And those who are Christ's have crucified the flesh with its passions and desires

If we live in the Spirit, let us also walk in the Spirit.

EMPOWERMENT BY THE SPIRIT

Biblical fasting is one of God's remedies to assist us in putting to death the lustful desires of the flesh. Fasting also helps empower us and enables us to live in the overcoming power of the Holy Spirit.

As you pursue a biblical fast, consider keeping a personal balance sheet to evaluate and consider how much time, energy, thought, devotion and money is spent on anything and everything other than the pursuit of righteousness, faith, love and peace with other Christians. You may be surprised at the accounting. I was.

You may already know the balance sheet is waning based on your current lifestyle. On the other hand, you may have been a Christian for years and find yourself surrounded by Christians, but you have never taken to heart whether you are pursing agape love and fellowship with a pure heart.

For purposes of a self-evaluation, take the first 12 hours of your day as a guide. Honestly consider how much of your mental thoughts, evaluations, assessments and energies are being directed at anything other than righteousness, faith, love and peace in your business deliberations, in your ethical deliberations and in your relational deliberations.

The lusts of the world are not only the obvious outward lusts, but also consist of inward motivations and strivings that are contrary to the will of God. When you fast, ask God to reveal the inward motivations and strivings that have been competing with His purposes in your life. Then ask Him to purify and sanctify your motives and intents.

Make a conscious effort to be sensitive to the Holy Spirit in pinpointing any unconscious lusts and inner strivings. Be honest. Then, make a conscious and decisive effort to redirect your will, thoughts, time, energy, emotions, devotion and money away from lust. Ask the Holy Spirit to redirect you in a pro-active pursuit of righteousness, love and peace.

Scriptures to meditate on include Philippians 1:9-11, Philippians 4:8-9 and Colossians 3.

It is impossible to fulfill the first and foremost commandment if you allow lust to remain in any area of your life. If lust remains, it will cloud your vision and keep *agapao* love from operating in and through your life. Lust will tell you it can live along side of *agapao* love; however, *agapao* love will **never** allow lust to live along side of it. *Agapao* love simply cannot live with lust.

Lust is one of the most deceptive feelings and emotions known to man. We often proclaim that we "love a person" when that proclamation is based entirely on lust. The true test of love vs. lust is found in the Word of God. 1 John 2:15 states that if you love the world and the things of the world, the love of God is not in you.

Ask yourself, "Do I love the world and the things of the world?" If you do, you do not have the love of God operating in your life, and if you do not have the love of God operating in your life, you cannot fulfill the first and foremost commandment of God. If you cannot fulfill the first and foremost commandment of God, you do not know God the way He desires you to know Him, and God's love has not been perfected and matured in you.

If you pursue the world and its lusts over the love of God, you will forfeit eternal rewards intended to be given to you. In Revelation 22:12

Jesus Christ says, "And behold, I am coming quickly, and My reward is with Me, to give to everyone according to his work."

The Greek word for "reward" is the word *misthos* and means compensation or recompense for service to God, divine rewards given for the moral quality of actions done in this lifetime. In 1 Corinthians 3:13-15, the Apostle Paul tells us that each one's works for the LORD will be revealed by fire to test it to see what sort of work it is. If anyone's works which he has built on endures, he will receive a reward, but if the work is burned, he will suffer loss, but he himself will be saved.

On the Day of Atonement, I was seeking the LORD, and He made a simple statement to me, "If you pursue My love in all things, you will receive the desires of your heart." When I considered these words, the Scripture that came to mind was Matthew 6:33:

> Seek first the Kingdom of God and His righteousness, and all things shall be added unto you.

The word "first" used in Matthew 6:33 is the Greek word *protos* and is generally spoken of in time and order and means the first in importance. The word "righteousness" is the Greek word *dikaiosune* and has many shades of meaning, but in this instance, it means righteousness regarding God and His divine law, where the heart is right with God or godliness. The first and foremost divine law in the LORD's Kingdom is to love. Therefore, seeking *agapao* love first in everything is the fulfillment of Matthew 6:33. When we put first-things first, all other things will then be added, not vice versa.

Whenever I see the word *all* in a Scripture, I take note. *All* is not a word of limitation. *All* is a recovery word and Matthew 6:33 is a recovery Scripture.

We can take Matthew 6:33 to the divine bank. Putting the law of love first is fulfilling Matthew 6:33. When we do this, God declares He will add everything else in our lives—the mark of *Divine Restoration.*

Ask the LORD to create in you a heart of love for your family, brothers and sisters in the faith and for the world. When your heart is filled love, everything in your life changes…everything! You begin to see the world through God's eyes and see that God desires to bring restoration and recovery to you, your family and the world and wants to use your life to do it. A Hebrew phrase for repairing the world is *Tikkum Olam.* *Tikkum* is derived from the Hebrew word *letaken,* meaning to fix or repair, and *Olam* is the Hebrew word for world.

This is what *agapao* love manifested will do: it will repair the world. It will repair breaches that sin has caused in your own life and will repair breaches that sin has caused in the lives of those around you. We are God's ambassadors and agents on Earth. We are the divine expression of the invisible God. God's divine expression of His *agapao* love was fully expressed to us when God the Father selflessly gave His Son to die for you and me. In addition, God the Son's divine expression of God the Father was fully expressed to us when God the Son selflessly endured the beatings, mocking and death by crucifixion death on the cross at Mt. Calvary.

These two expressions of love by God the Father and God the Son were given to bring restoration to this world. The divine power that allowed Jesus Christ to endure the physical pain of death and separation from His Father on the cross also allowed Him to be raised from the dead three days later. This same power force lives within every child of God. This power force is the Holy Spirit and is the power force that allows us to love others with unconditional love. The DNA of God is love.

If we each commit to follow the commandment to love, we are guaranteed to experience restoration. The Scripture declares emphatically,

"Love never fails."

—1 CORINTHIANS 13:8

This is a statement of guarantee. The word for "fails" is the Greek word *pipto* and means to fall to the ground, to fail or become void. In other words, 1 Corinthians 13:8 declares that *agape* love cannot ever, no matter the circumstance or situation, fall to the ground, fail or become void.

LET LOVE ABOUND

Pursue *agapao* love. Cultivate *agapao* love in your heart. Meditate on and allow the Holy Spirit to place inside your heart the truth that the *agapao* love you have pursued, will never return void or fail. This truth will transform your life.

A Scripture I pray that has brought the most amazing results in and around my life and circumstances is found in Philippians 1:9-11:

> And this I pray, that your love may abound still more and more in knowledge and all discernment,
>
> That you may approve the things that are excellent, that you may be sincere and without offense till the day of Christ,
>
> Being filled with the fruits of righteousness which are by Jesus Christ, to the glory and praise of God.

When the LORD directed me to pray this Scripture, after 10 days the most amazing things started happening. In the Spirit, I saw fortified foundations laid with cement begin to crack and break. The picture showed foundations that had not been laid with the love of Christ. These were spiritual foundations in the heart. Once I began to decree the *agapao* love of God to abound in my life and those around me, hardened hearts (cement foundations) began to crumble. Once these foundations began to crumble, I decreed the laying of a new foundation, one based on the *agapao* love of God.

The Apostle Paul tells us there is no other foundation that can be laid than that which is Jesus Christ and therefore, we are to be careful how we build on it:

> According to the grace of God which was given to me, as a wise master builder I have laid the foundation, and another builds on it. But let each one take heed how he builds on it.
>
> For no other foundation can anyone lay than that which is Jesus Christ.
>
> Now if anyone builds on this foundation with gold, silver, precious stone, wood, hay, straw,
>
> Each one's work will become clear; for the Day will declare it, because it will be revealed by fire, and the fire will test each one's work, of what sort it is.
>
> If anyone's work which he has built on it endures, he will receive a reward.
>
> If anyone's work is burned, he will suffer loss; but he himself will be saved, yet so as through fire.
>
> —1 CORINTHIANS 3:10-15

Consider the foundations you have laid and the building materials you have used to build on the foundation of Christ in your life.

Knowing that the LORD's fire will prove the worth or worthlessness of the building materials used, consider your life's aim and efforts up to this point. Be honest and sincere with the LORD. Don't be afraid to admit fault and begin building again with a new set of spiritual materials and tools. The Holy Spirit will be with you as the wise master craftsman to help you in each decision you make.

I encourage you to meditate on the Scriptures as you build on Christ's foundation. Proverbs Chapters 2, 3, 4 and 8 are filled with a plethora of wisdom and spiritual wealth. Wisdom was with God when He formed the world, and wisdom is the seminal trait in the LORD's master building plan.

> The LORD possessed me at the beginning of His way, before His works of old.
>
> I have been established from everlasting, from the beginning, before there was ever an earth.
>
> When there were no depths I was brought forth, when there were no fountains abounding with water.
>
> Before the mountains were settled, before the hills, I was brought forth;
>
> While as yet He had not made the earth or the fields, or the primal dust of the world.
>
> When He prepared the heavens, I was there, when He drew a circle on the face of the deep,
>
> When He established the clouds above, when He strengthened the foundations of the deep,
>
> When He assigned to the sea its limit, so that the waters would not transgress His command, when He marked out the foundations of the earth,

Then I was there beside Him as a master craftsman; and I was daily His delight, rejoicing always before Him,

Rejoicing in His inhabited world, and my delight was with the sons of men.

—PROVERBS 8:22-31

More riches follow:

Through wisdom a house is built, and by understanding it is established;

By knowledge the rooms are filled with all precious and pleasant riches.

A wise man is strong, Yes, a man of knowledge increases strength;

For by wise counsel you will wage your own war, and in the multitude of counselors there is safety.

—PROVERBS 24:3-6

Pursing *agape* love is the wisdom of God. Building your house on love is the plan of God, and loving God with all your heart is the Counsel of God that brings *Divine Restoration*. Love is God and God is love. Love never fails.

$\mathcal{C}$ONFRONTING MURDER

THE SIN OF UNRIGHTEOUS ANGER AND LASHON HARA

$\mathcal{Y}$ou don't often hear Christians speaking about murder. Many people think of murder in the Scriptures to consist solely of the physical act of killing another individual. However, the act of murder according to God is much broader. In fact, the Bible declares that murder consists of harboring unrighteous anger in your heart toward another person.[137] The Scripture also declares that murder comes from an evil tongue. In Hebrew, this tongue is called *Lashon Hara*.[138] The sin of murder in heart and tongue is so prevalent it can be called the "silent killer of everything good and righteous." God calls it murder.

The first act of unrighteous anger leading to murder in the Scriptures is found in Genesis and involves the first two siblings, Cain and Able. The account goes:

---

137. Matthew 5:21-22

138. Matthew 5:22, James 3:8

Now the man had relations with his wife Eve, and she conceived and gave birth to Cain, and she said, "I have gotten a manchild with the help of the LORD."

And again, she gave birth to his brother Abel. And Abel was a keeper of flocks, but Cain was a tiller of the ground.

So it came about in the course of time that Cain brought an offering to the Lord of the fruit of the ground.

Abel, on his part also brought of the firstlings of his flock and of their fat portions. And the LORD had regard for Abel and for his offering;

But for Cain and for his offering He had no regard. So Cain became very angry and his countenance fell.

Then the LORD said to Cain, "Why are you angry? And why has your countenance fallen?

"If you do well, will not your countenance be lifted up? And if you do not do well, sin is crouching at the door, and its desire is for you but you must master it."

Cain told Abel his brother. And it came about when they were in the field, that Cain rose up against Abel his brother and killed him.

—GENESIS 4:1-8, NASB

Notice how the sin of murder begins. Abel brought an acceptable offering of the first fruit of his flock, and the LORD "had regard for Abel and his offering," meaning the LORD looked upon the offering and considered it righteous.

Cain, on the other hand, brought an offering from the ground, but the LORD did not have regard for his offering. Therefore, Cain became angry that his brother's offering was righteous and acceptable, but his was not. The word "angry" used in this Scripture is the Hebrew word *charah,* which means to grow warm, to blaze up in anger, zeal, jealousy or to burn or become vexed. As a result of this vexing state of jealousy, Cain murdered his brother Abel.

Cain's *charah* (anger) at his brother was not anger based on righteousness, but was anger based on unrighteousness. God calls this type of anger murder and told Cain that his anger needed to be mastered. The word "master" is the Hebrew word *marshal,* which means to rule or have dominion over. God counseled Cain to master, rule over and have dominion over his unrighteous anger. However, instead of mastering his unrighteous anger and humbling himself before the LORD, he turned away from God. When Cain turned away from God, his unrighteous anger was loosed without restraint. Unrestrained, unrighteous anger led to the first murder and the shedding of innocent blood.

While writing this chapter, I had a dream. In the dream, an individual looked me in the eye and said with sincerity, "I am going to kill you."

In response I asked, "But why do you want to kill me?"

The person answered, "Because I am jealous of you. You have gotten to make choices in your life that I was not able to make. Had I been able to do my life over again, I would not have made the choices I made and be in the situation I am in."

This woman had lived under a web of lies. As a result, her heart had grown angry at God. The anger developed into a heart of jealousy, leading to murderous thoughts.

Unrighteous anger, leading to jealousy causes the murder of dreams, the murder of hope and even the murder of life. The Commandment of

God states, "Thou shall not murder."[139] This Commandment prohibits the act of physical murder. But murder can extend in thought and word, through unrighteous anger and destructive insults. God says,

> "You shall not go about as a talebearer {slanderer} among your people, nor shall you stake a stand against the life of your neighbor: I am the LORD.
>
> "You shall not hate your brother in your heart. You shall surely rebuke your neighbor, and not bear sin because of him.
>
> "You shall not take vengeance, nor bear any grudge against the children of your people, but you shall love your neighbor as yourself: I am the LORD."
>
> —LEVITICUS 19:16-18

The Apostle James summarizes the deadly poison of murder found in the tongue when he states,

> And the tongue is a fire, a world of iniquity. The tongue is so set among our members that it defiles the whole body, and sets on fire the course of nature; and it is set on fire by hell.
>
> For every kind of beast and bird, of reptile and creature of the sea is tamed and has been tamed by mankind.
>
> But no man can tame the tongue. It is an unruly evil, full of deadly poison.
>
> With it we bless our God and Father, and with it we curse men, who have been made in the similitude of God.

---

139. Exodus 20:13

Out of the same mouth proceed blessing and cursing. My brethren, these things ought not to be so.

—JAMES 3:6-10

James declares that the untamed tongue is a fuel of fire, full of evil and deadly poison, and when left unrestrained causes the cursing of man.

During a time of prayer, the Holy Spirit asked me to turn around and put my back toward the LORD. As I turned my back toward the LORD, He said,

> "This is what your generation has done toward Me. They have turned their back to Me. Tell this generation that I am not the cause of their anger. Tell this generation that it was not Me that caused their injuries and injustices. Tell this generation that I am not the One to be angry with. Tell them I am innocent."

These words came from the heart of God pleading for His own vindication, as if He needed vindication. God is not the cause of man's unrighteous anger, nor is He the cause or creator of lies covering people that have made the heart of the righteous sad. We have all turned our backs to God. As a result, we have acquired unrighteous anger toward our fellow man and toward God. This is sin and unacceptable to God.

You don't have to look far to see men and women of all ages looking with distain, anger and resentment in their eyes at their fellow man. It is on the news, in the streets, in our homes, in our families and even prevalent among our own brethren. Yet how we treat others is how we treat God, because man was made in the image of God.[140] Speaking

---

140. Genesis 1:27, James 3:6-10

against another person from a heart with unrighteous anger tarnishes the image of God.

Jesus Christ affirmed that murder not only include unrighteous anger in our heart toward our brother, but also includes destructive words directed toward our brother:

> You have heard that the ancients were told, "You shall not commit murder" and "whoever commits murder shall be liable to the court." But I say to you that everyone who is angry with his brother shall be guilty before the court; and whoever says to his brother, "*Raca*" ("You good-for-nothing") shall be guilty before the supreme court; and whoever shall say, "You fool," shall be guilty enough to go into the fiery hell.
>
> If therefore, you are presenting your offering at the altar, and there remember that your brother has something against you, leave your offering there before the altar, and go your way; first be reconciled to your brother, and then come and present your offering.
>
> —MATTHEW 5:21-24, NASB

In this Scripture, the word "angry" is the word *orgizo* which means to provoke to anger and describes a passion that is furious and raging, with a desire for revenge. Jesus Christ says that if you are angry at your brother and desire revenge, you are guilty of murder. Further, if you call your brother "*Raca*" an expression of contempt for someone and calling the person worthless, you are also guilty of murder.

The Scriptures also state that if you have hatred in your heart toward your brother, you are guilty of the sin of murder. The Apostle John instructs,

In this the children of God and the children of the devil are manifest: Whoever does not practice righteousness is not of God, nor is he who does not love his brother.

For this is the message that you have heard from the beginning, that we should love one another,

Not as Cain who was of the wicked one and murdered his brother. And why did he murder his brother? Because his works were evil and his brother's righteous.

Do not marvel, my brethren, if the world hates you.

We know that we have passed from death to life, because we love the brethren. He who does not love his brother abides in death.

Whoever hates his brother is a murderer, and you know that no murderer has eternal life abiding in him.

—1 JOHN 3:10-15

The issue of unrighteous anger and hate is an issue of the heart. Luke 6:45 admonishes us that out of the abundance of the heart, the mouth speaks and a good man out of the good treasure of his heart brings forth good; but an evil man out of the evil treasure of his heart brings forth evil. Unrighteous anger and hate is evil and brings forth evil treasure from the heart.[141]

LASHON HARA

The purpose of an Isaiah 58 fast is to allow God to produce in our lives an inward change of heart. The mouth will speak that which is in the heart. Jesus Christ told us that murder originates or begins in

---

141. Matthew 12:33-37

the heart and then flows out of the heart to the mouth through the releasing of destructive statements. These destructive statements are known in Hebrew as originating from evil tongue or *Lashon hara*.

Lashon hara is used to describe evil speech as well as gossip. It is also defined as defaming a person by revealing negative truthful details about the person to others, which is commonly known as slander.

The Apostle James spends an entire chapter speaking about the dangers of the tongue.[142] James instructs us not to speak against one another as brethren, for he who speaks against a brother or judges his brother "speaks against the law and judges the law."[143] The Greek word for "speak against" used in James 4:11 is the word *katalaleo* and means to slander or speak evil of. The word also includes backbiting.

> But there is only one Lawgiver and Judge, the One who is able
> to save and to destroy, but who are you to judge your neighbor?
>
> —JAMES 4:12

James reminds us that we are not the Judge or the Lawgiver, but that right has been given only to Christ. As such, we have no right to slander or speak evil against a brother, for in doing so, we become judges whom God did not appoint.

Jesus Christ declared that no offering or gift you bring to the altar will be acceptable if you have revenge in your heart or through your words and destructive insults you have contempt for your brother.[144] The Scripture declares that you must first be reconciled to your brother before your offering will be received. The word "brother" used in

---

142. James 3

143. James 4:11

144. Matthew 5:23-24

Matthew 5:24 is the word *adelphos* and includes not only a brother from the same father or mother, but also a near relative, one of equal rank, a disciple of Christ, one of the same faith or *any* fellow man.

God commands us to leave our offering at the altar and first be reconciled to our brother.[145] The phrase "be reconciled" in Matthew 5:24 is the Greek word *diallasso* and means to change one's own feelings toward, to reconcile oneself to or to cause a state of peace to be between two persons. Before your offering and gift will be acceptable to God, you should confess and seek the removal of unrighteous feelings and attitudes toward your brother.

How many of us are guilty of bringing offerings to God with hate and contempt in our heart toward our brother? When we seek to give God an offering from our hands when our heart is not right with God, the offering is not accepted by God.

Apart from a change of heart, apart from the removal of unrighteous anger, no amount of fasting, no amount of offering, no amount of good works will be acceptable to God or bring the desired and sought-after restoration.

Consider probing your heart and intentions by asking yourself these questions:

1. Am I continuing to justify unrighteous anger toward any brother?

2. Am I a gossip, slanderer, talebearer?

3. Do I repeat negative truthful facts or details about others?

If you answer "yes" to any of the above questions, stop. According to the Scriptures, no offering will be acceptable before God with these sins in your heart. Ask God to show you where you have been judging your

---

145. Ibid

brother or yourself in unrighteousness. If the Holy Spirit shows you this sin, ask the LORD to change your heart and give you a heart of love toward your brother. The purpose of an acceptable fast is to "take away the yoke from your midst, the pointing of the finger and speaking wickedness" so that when you call the LORD will answer, and when you cry, the LORD will say, "Here I am."

When the Holy Spirit reveals unrighteous anger, ask the LORD to grant you the grace to repent and give you a change of heart. Then, ask the LORD to bless and restore to your brother everything good that has been withheld from him because of your unrighteous anger toward him. If you have difficulty blessing your brother, ask the LORD to reveal why? You may have jealousy toward your brother in your heart. If this is so, repent and ask God to remove every trace of jealousy. Jealousy is like a poisonous cancer; it can destroy your life.

We are Christ's ambassadors on Earth with the purpose of establishing His righteousness in all realms of influence. When we live with a transformed heart of righteousness and speak from a transformed heart of righteousness, we become agents of transformation and influence in our families, cities and nation.

It is the will of God that our lives and offerings be acceptable in righteousness.[146] It is not God's will that we bring vain and worthless offerings to the LORD that have no merit or value. To the contrary, our Father knows we desperately desire to bring Him an offering made and formed in righteousness, or we would not be fasting and seeking a change of mind and heart.

Decide today to seek a radical transformation of heart and tongue toward your brother. As your speech becomes filled with grace and seasoned with salt, your tongue will no longer be used as an agent that

---

146. Malachi 3:3

caused a breach, but rather can be used as an agent for repairing the breach.

Here is a Scripture to consider praying in this regard:

> "The Lord GOD has given me the tongue of the learned, that I should know how to speak a word in season to him who is weary.
>
> He awakens Me morning by morning, He awakens My ear to hear as the learned."
>
> —ISAIAH 50:4

The word "learned" is the Hebrew word *limmuwd,* which means a disciple, a follower or one taught. Ask the LORD to grant you the tongue of the *learned* because you have chosen to be a disciple, a follower. Ask the LORD to grant you an ear to hear as the *learned* so you may obey Him in all things.

"TO KILL, STEAL AND DESTROY"

God desires our generation to war against the enemy of murder in our hearts, in our nation and in the other nations on Earth. Our generation has seen the rise of the sin of murder and its devastating effects through the legalization of abortion. The U.S. Supreme Court case that legalized abortion, *Roe v. Wade* (1973), was a case whose inception and beginnings we now understand was based on a web of lies perpetuated on the Court. But *Roe v. Wade* was not the beginning of murder in our nation; it was only the "eye opening" case that "legalized" the killing of babies and caught our attention. The seeds of murder in our nation began many years prior to 1973.

I was given a video called *180 Degrees,* which is narrated by Ray Comfort. The video depicts interviews taken on the street of this nation asking individuals if they knew of Adolph Hitler. He then likens the Holocaust to the present-day abortion crisis and through thought provoking questions begins to obtain from these same individuals a "180 Degree" turn in the way they viewed abortion.

After I viewed the video, I contemplated whether there could be a correlation between the Holocaust and the legalization of abortion in America? As an attorney, I cannot provide counsel to bring solutions to a problem until I first understand the inception of the problem. The same is also true for understanding spiritual matters. It is important to first identify the root of the sin and then determine where/how the sin entered in order to remove the legal rights and dominion of the sin.

I began by looking at the history of the immigration of individuals of Jewish descent and other Europeans to America. In doing so, I came across the word, *Eugenics*. A known social movement in the 1880s, eugenics claimed to improve the genetic features of human populations through what is called "selective breeding and sterilization," based on the idea that it is possible to distinguish between superior and inferior people in a society. In my research, I learned that it was common knowledge that eugenics was practiced in the United States years before eugenics programs were practiced in Nazi Germany. In fact, it has been ascribed that the United States programs provided much of the inspiration for the Nazi Germany eugenics programs.

The history of eugenics in the U.S. can be read extensively on the Internet. It appears that this evil and murderous vein of thought that began in the 1880s was received in the United States and flourished through extensive funding from foundations. It was also widely received by the academic community, which offered course curriculums in eugenics. There was even an association begun in 1906 called the "American Breeder's Association." One of the most prominent feminist advocates for the eugenic platform was a woman who was a leader in the American birth control movement.

The correlation between the inception of and flourishing of this evil vein of murderous thought in the United States and the Holocaust cannot be ignored. Nor can the fact that the eugenic platform was promoted by a woman whose agenda was to "control birth"—abortion.

Because murder begins in the heart, unless the heart changes, mouth and tongue, deed and action will not change. Satan is a murderer and the father of lies. Jesus Christ declared the following:

> You are of your father the devil, and the desires of your father you want to do. He was a murderer from the beginning, and does not stand in the truth, because there is no truth in him. When he speaks a lie, he speaks from his own resources, for he is a liar and the father of it.
>
> —JOHN 8:44

Satan is clear in his motivations: to kill, steal and destroy.[147] He kills, steals and destroys individuals, families and nations through breeding and perpetuating webs of lies formed by hate and unrighteous anger toward each other; the sin that leads to murder. God is love, the opposite of hate.[148] Because God is love, He has only one motivation, to love. God is also all truth and all life. Jesus Christ said,

> I am the way, the truth and the life. No one comes to the Father except through Me.
>
> —JOHN 14:6

> I am the resurrection and the life.
>
> —JOHN 11:25

---

147. John 10:10
148. 1 John 4:8

The thief does not come except to steal, and to kill and to destroy. I have come that they may have life, and that they may have it more abundantly.

—JOHN 10:10

SEEKING IS THE KEY

So what are we to do? Restoration to our own hearts, our families, and nation comes when we ask God to grant us forgiveness for allowing the iniquity of murder to be formed and flourish in our lives and in our hearts. Restoration begins when we seek God for a change of heart toward each other. The purpose of an Isaiah 58 fast is a change of heart toward God and each other.

Ask God to show you the sin of murder in and around you. Then seek sincere repentance for the sin. Ask God to forgive you of any race and class structure or division cultivated in your heart. Ask God to forgive you of any pride, arrogance or self-seeking. As we seek forgiveness for allowing unrighteous anger and jealousy to flourish in our hearts, restoration will flow. As we seek forgiveness for allowing murder in word, tongue, thought and deed to infiltrate our hearts and our nation, restoration will flow. If we each do our part, we can change the future of our heritage and reverse what former generations have done or failed to do. Divine Restoration—this is the LORD's passionate quest.

Consider the wisdom of God in giving our generation the medical invention of a sonogram. Sonograms allow us to see into the womb of a woman to reveal to us a mystery of God that was once hidden: the formation of a human life in the womb of the mother. The sonogram is God's mercy to our generation, so that those who cannot "see" may be able to "see" and turn from the lies of deception and deceit they have believed to the truth.

Can we do something to turn this situation around? Yes, we can each do something, and that something is to ask God to change our hearts and change our minds about ourselves and each other. If we will seek a change of heart about the sin of murder, restoration will flow, one-by-one, family-by-family, nation-by-nation. Restoration is a fire that can be caught. Once you have it, it is desired by others around you. God has promised if we sincerely seek to know and do His ways, He will bring a speedy healing and recovery to our lives and our land.[149] It is God who will turn our sordid past into a morally excellent and glorious future for our children, grandchildren and future generations.

One day, the LORD gave a vision regarding the sins of jealousy, hate, malice and murder. In the vision, I saw these sins, and although these sins have caused unspeakable horror, sorrow and heartache in every generation, I also saw the unmatchable power of the blood of Jesus Christ that was sent to pardon, cleanse, override and repair every breach caused by these sins. In the vision, the destruction and pain caused by these sins paled grossly in weight by comparison to the heaviness of the weight of the glory found in the pardoning blood of Jesus Christ. In fact, there was no comparison between the two. The pardoning blood of Jesus Christ and its cleansing and restorative power far exceeds, outweighs, outperforms and overcomes the vilest evil imaginable to man.[150] Exactly the reason why Jesus Christ encouraged His followers to be of good cheer, for "I have overcome the world."[151]

God's formula of fasting according to the precepts outlined in Isaiah 58 gives God the opportunity to reveal the vilest of sin and prepares a way for the pardoning and restorative power of the blood of Jesus Christ to have its full effect. The blood of Jesus Christ is the only vein

---

149. Isaiah 58:8

150. Hebrews 9:11-28, Ephesians 1:7, 1 John 1:7

151. John 16:33

and artery to restoration and is the reason this book is called *Divine Restoration.*

Divine Restoration can only be accomplished by and through Divine blood; there is no other blueprint or plan. The blood of Jesus Christ is fully and completely able to cleanse the conscience of our lives, our nation and the other nations on Earth. This is Counsel of God and the plan of God for *Divine Restoration.*

CONDEMNATION: THE ARCH ENEMY TO THE GOSPEL OF GRACE

On Christmas Day while speaking in a prison, the LORD said, "There are veils of condemnation on the hearts of My people; therefore, they are unable to hear from Me, believe Me or see who they are in Me. Explain that when people are given My Spirit, I come to live in their hearts. I AM all grace and truth. I AM not condemnation, for "I did not come into the world to condemn the world but that the world through Me might be saved."[152]

God desires to remove veils (coverings) of condemnation from the hearts of His children so we can hear from God, believe in God and live out the fullness of our identity as joint heirs in Christ.

---

152. John 3:17

There is therefore now no condemnation to those who are in Christ Jesus, who do not walk according to the flesh, but according to the Spirit.

For the law of the Spirit of life in Christ Jesus has made me free from the law of sin and death.

For what the law could not do in that it was weak through the flesh, God did by sending His own Son in the likeness of sinful flesh, on account of sin. He condemned sin in the flesh,

That the righteous requirement of the law might be fulfilled in us who do not walk according to the flesh but according to the Spirit.

—ROMANS 8:1-4

The Greek word for "condemnation" is the word *katakrima* and means an adverse sentence. It is derived from the word *katafrino,* which means to condemn or to have judgment against. The Apostle Paul declares there is **no condemnation** or adverse sentence to those who are in Christ and those who walk according to the Spirit. Condemnation or an adverse sentence begins and ends with the flesh, not the Spirit. The Spirit of God cannot be condemned. Only the carnal, natural flesh is condemned. The Spirit of God gives life to us, not condemnation. The carnal, natural flesh profits or is valued as nothing.[153]

Condemnation in the heart is a barrier to receiving the LORD's gracious plan of restoration. A friend told me during her fast that the LORD instructed her to read this chapter many times for her to obtain a full understanding of the extent of condemnation operating in her life. She was amazed at how much condemnation had been accepted and thriving in her heart.

---

153. John 6:63

Isaiah 58:9-10 states:

> Then you shall call, and the Lord will answer; you shall cry and He will say, "Here I am. If you take away the yoke from your midst, the pointing of the finger and speaking wickedness,
>
> If you extend your soul to the hungry and satisfy the afflicted soul, then your light shall dawn in the darkness, and your darkness shall be as the noonday."

The pointing of the finger described by Isaiah is likened to falsely accusing the brethren. Falsely accusing the brethren originates from a heart of condemnation. Likewise, speaking wickedness is equated to stirring up accusations against another. Both actions, pointing the finger and speaking wickedness, amount to issuing an adverse sentence against another. Both actions proceed from a heart of condemnation.

The LORD says that if we stop pointing of the finger and speaking wickedness, then the oppressive yokes we have created from our actions will be removed. When the oppressive yoke is removed, "light shall dawn in the darkness and darkness shall be as the noonday."

Restoration cannot be fully experienced when condemnation remains in the heart. Therefore, we must identify and battle to remove seeds of this destructive enemy. Condemnation is that ugly voice inside our mind and heart, the voice of a critic, the voice of the accuser, the voice of the enemy. I honestly admit, I have not met one individual in the Body of Christ who does not have some form of condemnation in their heart. Condemnation is one of most prevalent and least addressed and spoken of barriers and obstructions to restoration. This fact hurts the heart of God. God desperately desires the veil of condemnation to be removed from the heart of His children.

In simple terms, there are two kinds of condemnation. The first is condemnation directed outward toward others or by others toward you. The second is self-condemnation, which is directed inward toward yourself. Both are sin, and both are opposed to and work against the Spirit of grace in your life.

Like most enemies, some are obvious, and others are more subtle. Condemnation appears in very subtle forms. Often, we have knowingly or unknowingly accepted condemnation in our heart and not been challenged to eliminate it. Acceptance of condemnation in our lives can be likened to living with a silent enemy—an enemy you have lived with for so long that you don't even realize you are living with an enemy. Jesus Christ came to destroy every work of darkness—condemnation is a work of darkness that must be destroyed.

The following is a non-exhaustive list of some characteristics of condemnation. If you find yourself identifying with any of these characteristics, ask the Holy Spirit to reveal any area of condemnation you may have in your life.

Characteristics of those who condemn include:

- a critical spirit and judgmental attitude

- a lack of mercy and compassion

- a lack of love

- an inability to "tolerate" people

- being quick to judge

- being quick to find fault

- pointing out error and mistakes in others without offering a solution

- demonstrating curt, quick-tempered, harsh, unkind behavior

- being unhelpful and unthankful

- being bitter, malicious, envious or wanting to get even

- pointing the finger of blame and fault-finding

- being unforgiving

- walking in pride or arrogance

Characteristics of those who self-condemn include:

- judge themselves harshly

- have trouble forgiving self

- inability to believe God's goodness should come to them

- feel unworthy before God

- have trouble believing God's promises are for them

- have difficulty receiving and acting by faith in God's Word

- have a victim mentality

- dislike themselves, show self-loathing and self-criticism

- have difficulty loving themselves and others

- have trouble trusting God

- believe they deserve suffering

- take on false guilt for things they did not do, take on the guilt of perpetrators around them

- feel responsible for the sins of others close to them

Neither of these lists are exhaustive but aid in identifying the characteristics of condemnation. How do you know you have condemnation operating in your life? Ask yourself some questions:

1. Am I *actively* growing in the Word of God? Condemnation keeps you from growing in faith.

2. Do I find myself being *transformed* into Christ's image and likeness, wearing His righteousness and walking in His mercy and love toward others?

3. Do I have *fullness* of joy?

4. Am I able to *receive* and *give* Christ's love and forgiveness?

5. Do I find myself *more* merciful and *less* judgmental of others who are different than me?

6. Do I *accept* myself and *allow* myself to love who God created me to be in a way that allows me to love "me" and love others?

7. Do I *hear* the Holy Spirit speak to me *in love and do I receive the words spoken*?

8. Do I *accept and receive* the promises of God given in His Word as promises directed to me?

9. Can I *receive, hear and act on* the Word of God by faith for myself and my own circumstances?

10. Do I really *believe* that God is for me and does my life reflect this belief?

11. Do I *freely* extend God's grace and love to others and myself, or do I place conditions on God's grace and love?

12. Do I offer and *allow* God's unconditional grace to flow through me to others and to myself?

13. Are my prayers *full of faith,* knowing they are answered "yes" and "amen" before I utter them off my lips?

14. Do *I believe* God loves me and has a good plan for me and does it show in my life of active faith?

15. Do *I believe* God wants me to be restored and made whole and does it show in my life through receiving Christ's love?

If you answered "No" to any of the above questions, seek the LORD regarding condemnation in your heart. Everyone has had some form of condemnation in his or her heart until that area has been surrendered to the LORD's grace and truth. When the Spirit of God lives inside of you at your new birth, you were not instantaneously freed from condemnation in your heart. The heart must be cultivated like a garden. Condemnation can be likened to a weed in the garden of the heart. It must be rooted out or it can grow and take over the garden.

The key for success over this enemy is to identify its workings and take the necessary precautions not to allow this enemy in your heart. The heart must be guarded and protected through understanding and receiving God's love and mercy into every area of your life, every loss, every failure, every disappointment and every rejection.

I was invited to a Christian congregation. When the individuals stood up to worship, I stood up as well. The moment I stood up; a spiritual wall came up in front of me. Immediately, I inquired of the LORD what the wall represented. The LORD said, "It is a wall of condemnation. There is condemnation in this place. You are not to receive the words spoken here." I reverently and quietly left the gathering and prayed for the congregation.

The LORD desperately desires His children to hear His voice, receive His love, walk in the power of the Holy Spirit and understand and embrace our adoption in Him as sons and daughters, joint heirs in Christ. Romans 8:14-17 states,

> For as many as are led by the Spirit of God, these are the sons of God.
>
> For you did not receive the spirit of bondage again to fear, but you received the Spirit of adoption by whom we cry out, "Abba, Father."
>
> The Spirit Himself bears witness with our spirit that we are children of God,
>
> And if children, then heirs—heirs of God and joint heirs with Christ, if indeed we suffer with Him, that we may also be glorified together.

The LORD is serious that His children know their full inheritance in Him as sons and daughters. Jesus Christ desperately wants us free from condemnation in our heart so we can live in His grace and truth and have full, unhindered communion with Him and one another in our most holy faith.

Condemnation is a spirit of bondage and will produce fear. 1 John 3:5 states that the reason Christ Jesus manifested Himself on Earth was that He might destroy the works of the devil. The word "destroy" in this Scripture is the Greek word *luo,* which means to dissolve, loose, melt, unbind or untie one who is bound in sin. Condemnation is a work of the devil that Christ Jesus came to dissolve, loose, melt, unbind and untie in our lives.

The Apostle Paul prayed in Ephesians 3:14-21 that we would each know the encompassing love of God and that we would be filled with all the fullness of God:

> For this reason I bow my knees to the Father of our Lord Jesus Christ,

From whom the whole family in heaven and earth is named,

That He would grant you, according to the riches of His glory, to be strengthened with might through His Spirit in the inner man,

That Christ may dwell in your hearts through faith; that you, being rooted and grounded in love,

May be able to comprehend with all the saints what is the width and length and depth and height—

To know the love of Christ which passes knowledge; that you may be filled with all the fullness of God.

Now to Him who is able to do exceedingly abundantly above all that we ask or think according to the power that works in us.

To Him be the glory in the church by Christ Jesus to all generations, forever and ever. Amen.

The word "fullness" is the Greek word *pleroma* and means the full measure, copiousness, plentitude and emphasizes completion. When we are filled with the full measure of Christ, we experience His love for us and can freely give His love to others. In this love, barriers of condemnation are removed. In this love, Christ's grace and truth is received. In this love, we obtain our inheritance. In this love is Divine Restoration.

PRAYER

Lord, I confess I have been living with condemnation a long time. I confess that it has taken root in my mind and heart. I am ready to depart from condemnation and have it completely removed from my heart. In Jesus' Name, I come out of agreement with condemnation.

I declare every root, fruit and tentacle of condemnation die, wither, dry up and be removed out of my heart.

I renounce, reject and disclaim every agreement I made knowingly or unknowingly with condemnation. I renounce, reject and disclaim any agreement with condemnation spoken over me or written against me.

I no longer accept condemnation in my heart. I decree that every adverse sentence spoken or written against me is now nullified, voided and cancelled. I decree reconciliation and restoration over myself and every person I have ever condemned.

I receive Your forgiveness and pardon through the blood of Jesus Christ to heal me and restore my heart. I allow the Spirit of grace to flow freely in and through my heart. Thank you, LORD, for loving me so very much. Thank you, LORD, for helping me keep seeds of condemnation out of my heart. Fill up my heart with Your love. Fill up my heart with Your mercy. Fill up my heart with Your truth.

AMEN

BREAKING THE CODE OF PRESUMPTION

$\mathcal{T}$he title to this chapter, *Breaking the Code of Presumption,* was chosen because a code is a message in secret form and remains hidden until it is known. Presumption is a sin that can be likened to a code, it is masked in such a way that it lies secret and hidden. Presumption is one of the deadliest and most grievous of sins. It is a sin that, when left hidden, will ruin your earthly life and severely limit your eternal inheritance. It is a sin that will perpetuate a web of lies and feed on a web of lies because presumption is founded on falsehoods, irreverence and rebellion to God. King David plead with the LORD to restrain him, hold him back from this sin:

Who can understand his errors? Cleanse me from secret faults.

Keep back Your servant also from presumptuous sins; Let them not have dominion over me. Then I shall be blameless, and I shall be innocent of great transgression.

Let the words of my mouth and the meditation of my heart be acceptable in Your sight, O LOR D, my strength and my Redeemer.

—PSALM 19:12-14

In this Psalm, King David acknowledges that certain errors are difficult to understand, and certain faults are or secret (*cathar*—hidden and concealed carefully). King David cites one sin—a sin that if left unattended would cause dominion over him and cause him great transgression. It is the sin of presumption.

The Hebrew word used in Psalm 19 for "presumption" is the word *zade* from the word *zuwd* which means to be proud, insolent, and arrogant. Presumptuous sins are comprised of defiant, arrogant and irreverent moral actions and attitudes toward God and His laws, commandments, statutes and judgments. Presumption is an attitude that assumes you are right when you are wrong.

Presumption is error in thought that causes people to think that they know better than God and, therefore, willfully and defiantly exalt their hearts, minds and actions above the LORD. Presumption leads to wrong thinking about yourself and God. Presumption rationalizes sin and, therefore, compromises grace. In relation to God and others, this sin causes offense through attitudes of arrogance and pride. Christians and non-Christians alike perpetuate this sin. Presumption causes stumbling, public disgrace and personal shame.

Jesus Christ addressed the sin of presumption when He rebuked the church of Laodicea, one of the seven churches identified in the book of Revelation. In Revelation 3:17, the LORD tells His church that although they say, "I am rich, have become wealthy, and have need of nothing," the LORD had another diagnosis: "Do you not know that you are wretched, miserable, poor, blind and naked?" The LORD counsels them to buy from Him gold having been refined in the fire, that they may be rich and may be clothed so that their shame would not be revealed.[154]

The sin of presumption in the Laodiceans blinded their eyes to the true state of their spiritual condition, a state of nakedness and personal shame. The people were not clothed in rich garments representing true works of righteousness, but rather had clothing consisting of works that were not acceptable to God. The Laodiceans were so deceived by the sin of presumption that they could not see their nakedness and shame and thus held a false belief in their spiritual condition.

Presumption is the sin that has robbed God of the honor, reverence and respect due His Name. If we are honest, we have all been partakers of this sin and drank from its cup. Its roots are pride and arrogance. Its covering is falsehoods. It smells of religion and tradition, lies and error. It is irreverent to the Word of God, the commandments of God, the statutes of God, the saints of God, the prophets of God and the Spirit of God. This sin causes people and nations to have no fear of God.

PRESUMPTION: "I KNOW BETTER THAN GOD"

King David manifested this sin when he attempted to bring the ark of God into Jerusalem without following the order designed by God, which required this most holy and sacred object to be carried on the shoulders of the priests, not carried on a cart by oxen. As a result, when the oxen carrying the ark stumbled and Uzzah, the priest, put out his hand to take hold of the ark, God struck him dead for his irreverence.[155]

---

154. Revelation 3:14-22

155. 2 Samuel 6:1-7

Presumption was evident again in King David's life when he ordered a census of Israel and Judah.[156] The prophet Gad came to King David to declare to him the choice of judgments offered by God for this sin. King David chose three days of plague on the land. As a result, 70,000 men of Israel and Judah died by the sword of an angel of the Lord.[157] Could this event be why King David wrote Psalm 19 and plead with God to keep him from presumptuous sins?

King Saul manifested the sin of presumption, was rejected by God as king and summarily lost the throne and title as king of Israel. The LORD told King Saul to attack Amalek and "utterly destroy all that they have and do not spare them."[158] Rather than obey, King Saul exalted his own thoughts above God, rebelled and spared the Amalek king, along with the best of the sheep and oxen and "all that was good." As a result, the prophet Samuel was sent to King Saul to announce to him the verdict of the LORD for his presumptuous sin. Samuel said to King Saul,

> "Has the LORD as great delight in burnt offerings and sacrifices, as in obeying the voice of the LORD? Behold, to obey is better than sacrifice, and to heed than the fat of rams.
>
> "For rebellion is as the sin of witchcraft, and stubbornness is as iniquity and idolatry. Because you have rejected the word of the LORD, He also has rejected you from being king."
>
> —1 SAMUEL 15:22-23

Presumption is thinking you know better than God how to live. Therefore, you exalt your thoughts and ways over God's thoughts and

---

156. 2 Samuel 24:1

157. 2 Samuel 24:15

158. 1 Samuel 15:3

ways. Presumption is doing things your way and believing you can live without God and not reap dire consequences. Presumption is the master sin behind the sin of rebellion, as seen in the life of King Saul. Presumption is also the master sin behind the conditions described in Isaiah 59 and the reason the webs of falsehood and lies were proudly worn as garments over the people and the nation.

On Mt. Sinai God gave the prophet Moses Ten Commandments to give to the nation of Israel, Commandments to live by. These Commandments are absolute, immutable and unchangeable. Moses also gave the nation, laws, judgements and statutes. Breaking God's righteous mandates produce adverse consequences to individuals and nations. Isaiah metaphorically describes the consequences of departing from God's mandates:

> Therefore justice is far from us, nor does righteousness overtake us; we look for light, but there is darkness! For brightness, but we walk in blackness!

> We grope for the wall like the blind, and we grope as if we had no eyes; we stumble at noonday as at twilight; we are as dead men in desolate places.

> We all growl like bears, and moan sadly like doves; we look for justice, but there is none; for salvation, but it is far from us.

> For our transgressions are multiplied before You, and our sins testify against us; for our transgressions are with us, as for our iniquities, we know them:

> In transgressing and lying against the LORD, and departing from our God, speaking oppression and revolt, conceiving and uttering from the heart words of falsehood.

> Justice is turned back, and righteousness stands afar off; for truth is fallen in the street and equity cannot enter.

So truth fails and he who departs from evil makes himself a prey.

—ISAIAH 59:9-15

The word "transgression" used in Isaiah 59 is the Hebrew word *pasha* which means to break away from, offend or revolt against the LORD. King David prayed that the LORD would keep him from the sin of presumption because it causes *great* transgression.[159] In other words, presumption causes a person to break away from, offend, and revolt against the LORD.

In the last seventy years, various legal decisions have been issued by various courts in the United States. Some of these decisions have been driven by the sin of presumption and have been in direct rebellion to God. The rulings did not enforce God's laws but legalized the departure or breaking away from God's moral and righteous laws.

As a result, the decisions have one by one set in motion the weaving of webs over this nation so that justice, righteousness, truth and equity fails to enter the fabric of the nation. The same conditions described in Isaiah 59 are the same conditions the United States suffers from today. These conditions are prevalent not only the United States, but in every nation that has departed from and broken away from the righteous and moral laws given by the Creator of Earth and the Judge of all men. It is inevitable, when the courts or legal administration of any nation choose to execute laws that depart from or break away from the laws of God, these adverse conditions will be the result.

Ask the LORD to reveal any roots, tentacles or fruits of the sin of presumption operating in your life. If the LORD reveals any part of this sin, repent and ask for cleansing and reform. Be diligent to partner

---

159. Psalm 19:13

with the Holy Spirit to have this sin removed from your life. Left unchecked, this sin will cause you to remain in error, separated from God, thereby thwarting deliverance and restoration.

Consider making Psalm 19:12-14 part of your daily prayer request from the LORD:

> Who can understand his errors? Cleanse me from secret faults.
>
> Keep back Your servant also from presumptuous sins; let them not have dominion over me. Then I shall be blameless, and I shall be innocent of great transgression.
>
> Let the words of my mouth and the meditation of my heart Be acceptable in Your sight, O Lord, my strength and my Redeemer.

Psalm 119 is also a good Psalm to meditate upon. Psalm 119:9-15 tells how a young man can cleanse his way and keep from wandering from the LORD:

> How can a young man cleanse his way? By taking heed according to Your word.
>
> With my whole heart I have sought You; Oh, let me not wander from your commandments!
>
> Your word I have hidden in my heart, that I might not sin against You.
>
> Blessed are You, O LORD! Teach me Your statutes.
>
> With my lips I have declared all the judgments of Your mouth.
>
> I have rejoiced in the way of Your testimonies, as much as in all riches.

I will mediate on Your precepts, and contemplate Your ways. I will delight myself in Your statutes; I will not forget Your word.

Seeking the LORD with a whole heart and hiding the Word of God deep in your heart can keep you for the sin of presumption. Meditating on the Word of God gives good success and makes your way prosperous:

This Book of the Law shall not depart from your mouth, but you shall meditate in it day and night, that you may observe to do according to all that is written in it. For then you will make your way prosperous, and then you will have good success.

—JOSHUA 1:8

HOLY TERROR

In prayer, the LORD said to me, "Ask Me to give you a holy terror of Me. For when you understand the holy terror of Me, you will not commit presumptuous sin."

I had not likened God with "*holy* terror," but when I heard the LORD say these words, I understood what He meant. It is only when a person has a correct understanding of who God Almighty really is and not who we presumptuously think or believe that He is, that we will be kept from the sin of presumption. Several days later, I walked into a Jewish Synagogue. When I entered the Synagogue, I could feel the awesome presence of God I had never experienced in a physical place. When I walked by the sanctuary, I felt a reverent fear and terror of the LORD, so much so, I did not want to enter.

I later attended the Synagogue. When I walked into the sanctuary, a deep and profound reverence began to move up through my feet with every step I took. I left considering how Moses may have felt along with the children of Israel when they met God for the first time at Mt. Sinai.

At Mt. Sinai, God revealed Himself as the Lawgiver to an entire nation and spoke through a cloud that covered the mountain. God spoke from the mountain with lightning, thunder and voices.[160] His awesome voice shook the mountain, and the Israelites became afraid of Him, so much that they asked Moses to speak to God on their behalf because they feared God's voice and presence.[161]

As Christians, we don't approach God with a terror that pushes us from Him, but rather we draw near to God with a boldness that is offered through the grace of God's Son, Jesus Christ.[162] However, being justified before our Father by the grace of Jesus Christ should not eliminate, but rather provoke a greater need to have a *holy terror* of our Father and reverence for and toward His Holy Word.

A reverent fear of God and His Word will keep each of us, our children and our children's children from departing and breaking away from the law of God and keep us from becoming caught in a "web of lies" offered through the sin of presumption.

The fear of God is the beginning of wisdom.[163] Wisdom is the principal thing God beckons us to obtain, along with understanding.[164] As you pursue an Isaiah 58 fast, seek wisdom and understanding and ask the LORD to give you a holy and reverent fear of Him and His Word:

Who is the man that fears the LORD? Him shall He teach in the way He chooses.

---

160. Exodus 19:18-20

161. Exodus 20:18-21

162. Hebrews 4:16, 12:18-24

163. Proverbs 9:10

164. Proverbs 4:7

He himself shall dwell in prosperity, and his descendants shall inherit the earth. The secret counsel of the Lord is with those who fear Him, and He will show them His covenant.

—PSALM 25:12-14

In the fear of God, wisdom is found. Wisdom will preserve you, exalt you, promote you, bring honor to you and place on your head an ornament of grace and a crown of glory.[165] Wisdom brings *Divine Restoration* that is both personal and perpetual, restoration that will keep you, your children and your children's children from falling prey to the web of lies found in presumptuous sins.

---

165. Proverbs 4:5-10

$\mathcal{O}$BSTRUCTIONS TO RESTORATION

OBTAINING VICTORY IN THE UNSEEN REALM

$\mathcal{A}$n Isaiah 58 fast is designed to address barriers to restoration that exist in the heart and mind. It is also designed to address barriers to restoration that exist in the unseen realm: demonic princes and principalities sent to oppose your restoration. Lucifer, (aka Satan, the great dragon, the serpent of old, the devil) does not want you to obtain restoration. Through restoration, you and I can recover the glory originally purposed in our lives by our Father. Lucifer, however, can never recover the glory that God bestowed on him as the "anointed cherub that covers" the "seal of perfection, full of wisdom and perfect in beauty."[166] Lucifer's eternal fate is separation from God in hell, the place created by God as judgment for Lucifer and all other angels who defiantly rebelled against God and His authority.[167]

---

166. Ezekiel 28:12, 14

167. Matthew 25:14

Your restoration is vitally important to God. Your restoration vindicates the Name of the LORD. Restoration means that the LORD's glory, splendor, majesty and renown will be displayed in your life.[168] Restoration means you reclaim the original design of your Father: to express the manifestation of Christ's divine image, character and nature. Restoration exalts the redemption power of the blood of Jesus Christ over Satan's domination of sin and death.

When Jesus Christ died, He disarmed *principalities* (rulers) and *powers* (authorities) and made a public spectacle of them, triumphing over them in the cross.[169] The Greek word used in Colossians 2:15 for "rulers" is the word *arche* and means those with first or pre-eminent authority or dominion. The Greek word used for "powers" is the word *exousia* and means those with dominion, authority and rule. When Christ died on the cross, His death and blood paid the debt owed by Adam because of his sin and divinely restored man to his position of ruling and dominion authority on Earth. Christ's death, burial and resurrection caused a disarmament of the kingdom of Satan and his pre-eminent authority and dominion rule on Earth.

Jesus Christ granted the members of His Body the power (*exousia*— meaning delegated authority or right to act) to administer and enforce His Kingdom's dominion and rule on earth "as it is in heaven."

Jesus declared to Peter,

> And I also say to you that you are Peter, and on this rock I will build my church and the gates of Hades shall not prevail against it.

---

168. Isaiah 58:8

169. Colossians 2:15

And I will give you the keys of the kingdom of heaven and whatever you bind on earth will be bound in heaven and whatever you lose on earth will be loosed in heaven.

—MATTHEW 16:18-19

Keys represent authority in Scripture. Jesus Christ told Peter that as the appointed representative of God's Kingdom, Christ was granting to Peter dominion authority (*exousia*) and rule on Earth. This dominion authority is the original ruling authority that Adam was given in the Garden of Eden when God commanded him to subdue the earth and take dominion over it.[170]

When Jesus Christ died, was buried and rose from the grave, He reclaimed the ruling authority previously given to Adam. Having taken possession of the keys to all the realms of heaven and Earth, Jesus Christ re-issued to the Body of Christ the originally designed ruling authority and dominion in heaven and Earth that Adam had in the garden. This is divine restoration and one of the most spiritually significant transactions to occur on Earth—the King of the Universe, the Judge of all Men, proclaiming as a witness before heaven and Earth that His followers are now commissioned with His ruling dominion and authority to proclaim the Kingdom of God throughout Earth:

And Jesus came and spoke to them, saying:

All authority has been given to Me in heaven and on earth.

Go therefore and make disciples of all nations, baptizing them in the name of the Father and of the Son and of the Holy Spirit,

---

170. Genesis 1:28

Teaching them to observe all things that I have commanded you; and lo, I am with you always, even to the end of the age. Amen.

—MATTHEW 28:18-20

In Matthew 11:12, the Scripture declares that from the days of John the Baptist, the kingdom of heaven suffers violence and violent men take it by force. The Greek word for the phrase "by force" is the word *harpazo,* which means to snatch away suddenly and carries the sense of robbery and plunder. The Kingdom of God and the manifestation of His will on Earth has always been opposed by violent men, used by Satan, to rob and plunder all things that advance the Kingdom of God. These violent men are not operating from the Holy Spirit's influence, but rather from forces originating from the father of lies, Satan. Jesus Christ speaks of two seeds on Earth when He addressed the Pharisees, Abraham's seed and Satan's seed:

"I know that you are Abraham's descendants, but you seek to kill Me, because My word has no place in you.

"I speak what I have seen with My Father, and you do what you have seen with your father."

—JOHN 8:37-38

Jesus said to them, "If God were your Father, you would love Me, for I proceeded forth and came from God; nor have I come of Myself, but He sent Me.

"Why do you not understand My speech? Because you are not able to listen to My word.

"You are of your father the devil, and the desires of your father you want to do. He was a murderer from the beginning, and does not stand in truth, because there is no truth in him. When he speaks a lie, he speaks from his own resources, for he is a liar and the father of it.

—JOHN 8:42-44

As I began preparing for a fast during the season of Passover, the LORD spoke to me about the demonic forces in the spirit that sought to oppose the LORD's intended restoration of the children of Israel after their seventy year sentence in Babylonian captivity.[171] It was timely of the LORD to speak about spiritual opposition to restoration because Passover commemorates the LORD's first act of covenant restoration by delivering the nation of Israel from their oppressive captors in Egypt. During Passover, we celebrate the LORD as the deliverer from the bondage of sin and slavery. It is also a time we celebrate the LORD as the covenant *fulfilling* God. Exodus 6:3 states,

> I appeared to Abraham, to Isaac, and to Jacob as God Almighty, but by My name *LORD (Yahweh)* was not known to them.

God declares that He appeared to the patriarchs as the covenant *making* God, *El Shaddai* or God Almighty, but during the exodus God appeared to the children of Israel as the covenant *keeping* God, LORD or *Yahweh*. As the covenant keeper, *Yahweh* was going to do whatever it took to secure the deliverance of the nation of Israel from her captors, including showing signs and wonders in the heavens and earth. The Scripture says,

> Then Moses said to God, "Indeed, when I come to the children of Israel and say to them, 'The God of your fathers has sent me

---

171. Daniel 10

to you,' and they say to me, 'What is His name? What shall I say to them?'

And God said to Moses, "I AM WHO I AM." And He said, "Thus you shall say to the children of Israel, 'I AM has sent me to you.'"

Moreover God said to Moses, "Thus you shall say to the children of Israel: 'The LORD God of your father's, the God of Abraham, the God of Isaac, and the God of Jacob, has sent me to you. This is My name forever and this is My memorial to all generations.'"

—EXODUS 3:13-15

Leading up to the exodus, God hardened the king of Egypt's heart so He could multiply His signs and wonders in the land of Egypt.[172] The Scripture states his heart was hardened so God could lay his hand on Egypt and bring "My armies and My people out of Egypt by great judgments so the Egyptians will know that I am LORD."[173]

As part of the nation's deliverance, God executed judgment on all the gods of Egypt. These gods were not physical gods but spiritual, unseen demonic powers. In the Exodus account, we are given our first look into God dealing with "gods" in the unseen realm.

Fast forward a thousand plus years to the time of the prophet Daniel. Daniel was an exile in Babylon and served in the court of several kings during the nation of Israel's seventy-year sentence for disobedience. From 559-530 B.C., Cyrus ruled as king of Persia. During Cyrus' rule, the time for restoration had arrived, and a remnant who had survived the Babylonian exile returned to the land of Canaan and rebuilt Jerusalem.[174]

---

172. Exodus 7:3

173. Exodus 7:3-5

174. Isaiah 44:28-45:1

During Cyrus' third year of reign, Daniel fasted for three weeks. During the fast, Daniel received a vision of a man "clothed in white, whose waist was girded with gold of Uphaz! His body was like beryl, His face like the appearance of lightning, His eyes like torches of fire, His arms and feet like burnished bronze in color, and the sound of His words like the voice of a multitude."[175]

This man was an angel of the LORD sent to Daniel to declare to him the following:

> Then he said to me, "Do not fear, Daniel, for from the first day that you set your heart to understand, and to humble yourself before your God, your words were heard; and I have come because of your words.
>
> But the prince of the kingdom of Persia withstood me twenty-one days; and behold, Michael, one of the chief princes came to help me, for I had been left alone there with the kings of Persia.
>
> "Do you know why I have come to you? And now I must return to fight with the prince of Persia; and when I have gone forth, indeed the prince of Greece will come.
>
> "But I tell you what is noted in the Scripture of Truth. (No one upholds me against these, except Michael your prince)."
>
> —DANIEL 10:12-13, 20-21

These Scriptures give an account of certain unseen spiritual forces called princes and kings aligned to withstand and oppose Daniel receiving understanding of the time determined for the fulfillment of the promised restoration. The word for "prince" used here is the word *sar,* which means the head, captain, chief, master, ruler, general or leader.

---

175. Daniel 10:5-6

The spiritual opposition sent to oppose revelation getting to Daniel was a chief or head of the kingdom of the Persian nation. Why the Persian nation? Because Persia was the ruling nation on Earth. It was the unseen spiritual force ruling the Persian empire—the ruling empire—that sought to block and oppose the awesome revelation the LORD wanted to give Daniel regarding the end of days.

Another account that depicts opposition by unseen spiritual forces is found in Zechariah 3:1-5. In this courtroom scene, Satan is standing at the right hand of an angel of the LORD seeking to oppose the LORD because the time of restoration for the priests in Judah had been determined by God:

> Then he showed me Joshua the high priest standing before the angel of the LORD, and Satan standing at his right hand to oppose him.
>
> And the LORD said to Satan, "The LORD rebuke you Satan! The LORD who has chosen Jerusalem rebuke you! Is this not a brand plucked from the fire?"
>
> Now Joshua was clothed with filthy garments, and was standing before the Angel.
>
> Then He answered and spoke to those who stood before Him, saying, "Take away the filthy garments from him." And to him He said, "See, I have removed your iniquity from you, and I will clothe you with rich robes."
>
> And I said, "Let them put a clean turban on his head."
>
> So they put a clean turban on his head, and they put the clothes on him. And the Angel of the LORD stood by.

In this account, the exiled remnant and her priests were returning to Judah to begin the nation's restoration. However, before restoration could occur, the nation's spiritual leaders needed personal cleansing. In this courtroom scene, Satan stands directly opposed to the restoration required of the returning priests. But have no worry, the covenant keeping LORD, *Yahweh*, is present and directly rebukes Satan and enforces the decree of the Most High Court, a final, un-appealable judgment for divine cleansing for the returning priests.

RESTORATION BRINGS SPIRITUAL AND NATURAL OPPOSITION

Restoration will always bring spiritual opposition, but it will also bring natural opposition. The prophet Nehemiah faced natural opposition when he began to gather the Jewish remnant to rebuild the walls surrounding Jerusalem. The Scripture states that as soon as Sanballat heard that the children of Israel were rebuilding the wall, that he was furious, very indignant and mocked the Jews.[176] Not only did he mock the Jews, but also he sought to conspire against them to "weaken them" in their efforts.[177]

Likewise, the New Testament book of Acts of the Apostles is filled with account after account of opposition faced by the Church in proclaiming the gospel of grace.[178] The first martyr, Stephen, was a man full of faith who did great signs and wonders among the people.[179] He was opposed by former Roman slaves, but they were not able to resist the wisdom and the Spirit by which he spoke. Therefore, men stirred up

---

176. Nehemiah 4:1

177. Nehemiah 6:1-9

178. Acts 4, 5:17-42, 6:8-15, 7:54-60, 12, 14:5-7, 16:20-40

179. Acts 6:8

false witnesses against Stephen.[180] But Stephen, full of faith, addressed the high priests in the city with Holy Spirit power that caused their hearts to be cut. At the close of his preaching and amid his enemies, he observed the heavens open and saw the glory of God and Jesus Christ standing at the right hand of the Father. After seeing this open vision, men ran at Stephen, cast him out of the city and stoned him to death.[181]

Restoration will always bring opposition, but rest assured, Jesus Christ is standing for you.

In the early 1990s, I had an encounter with the LORD like that of Stephen. I received a phone call, the message of which released the forces of hell designed to kill. When the call came, I saw the heavens open, and the LORD stand up at His throne. I knew at that moment—even though all of hell had been assigned with vengeance, malice and hate, Jesus Christ was standing on my behalf.

I want to encourage you today: the same God who *stood* for Zechariah is the same God who *stood* for Stephen. He is also the same God who stands for you. God is for you. Heaven is for you, and no matter what hellish and demonic assignments have been assigned to hinder or opposed your restoration, —God Almighty, the King of Kings, Ruler of the Universe and Judge of all just men, is for you.

The LORD wants you to be wise to the unseen spiritual forces sent to oppose restoration. In order to contend against these forces, we must learn how to use the Word of God as our "mighty warring weapon and sharp double-edged sword."

> For we do not wrestle against flesh and blood, but against principalities, against powers, against the rulers of the darkness

---

180. Acts 6:9-13

181. Acts 7:54-59

of this age, against spiritual hosts of wickedness in the heavenly places.

Therefore, take up the whole armor of God that you may be able to withstand in the evil day, and having done all to stand.

Stand therefore, having girded your waist with truth, having put on the breastplate of righteousness,

And having shod your feet with the preparation of the gospel of peace;

Above all, taking the shield of faith with which you will be able to quench all the fiery darts of the wicked one.

And take the helmet of salvation, and the sword of the Spirit, which is the Word of God;

Praying always with all prayer and supplication in the Spirit, being watchful to this end with all perseverance and supplication for all the saints.

—EPHESIANS 6:12-18

The effective and successful soldier will always put on the full armor of God and go to battle using the sword of the Spirit: The Word of God. An effective soldier will have perseverance because it takes faithful perseverance to see the determined victory. The word "perseverance" in Ephesians 6:18 is the Greek word *proskarteresis* derived from the word *proskartereo,* which means to be consistently diligent, to give oneself continually to, to be strong and firm toward something or to remain.

Recall the patriarch Joseph. Psalm 105:18-19 describes that his feet were placed in fetters, and he was laid in irons, "until the time that his word came to pass, the word of the LORD tested him." The Hebrew word used for "word" is *emrah* in Psalm 105 is a word for commandment or speech. The Hebrew word for "tested" is the word *tsaraph* and means to purge away, melt, purify, refine or test. This word describes the purifying process of a refiner who heats metal to take away the dross.

Although Joseph had been rejected and sold by his brothers to become an Egyptian slave, and although he was falsely accused by his master's wife and sentenced unjustly to prison, Joseph remained faithful. During the years of trials and testing, Joseph did not waver in his commitment. Every circumstance he faced was meant by the LORD for his success and not for his calamity.

Although it may take years, the Counsel of the LORD will always lead you to restoration: restoration of relationships, restoration of family and restoration of your lineage line and legacy. However, as evidenced in Joseph's life, restoration does not happen overnight.

Joseph had to persevere through years of testing, trials and persecution in order to obtain the promised and determined end, which included not only restoration, but the LORD's vindication for the injustices done to him. During his life in Egypt, Joseph had to contend against the lies of others as well as contend against the unseen "gods of Egypt" that opposed the righteousness of God in his life. However, through every trial, God was with Joseph, and through every trial, Joseph stood firm in his commitment to God and determined not to sin.

Romans 8:28 declares that God works *all things* together for our good. As you look at Joseph's life, God was working the apparent negative circumstances together for Joseph's good and the good of the patriarchs' seed as well as for the good of the nations on Earth. God had promised Abraham that in his seed all the families on Earth would be blessed. Through Joseph's life, God was fulfilling His covenant promise to Abraham.[182]

---

182. Genesis 12:3

Stay persistent and steadfast as you contend against and battle the spiritual forces aligned against your restoration. Don't go to battle alone. The forces of evil and darkness are very real, and the battle tactics are fierce and unrelenting. You should have prayer covering and prayer support during your fast. Ask the LORD to bring you prayer partners or join a prayer group so you can engage in the power that comes from the prayer of agreement.

King David always inquired of the Counsel of the LORD to obtain the LORD's strategies before he went to war. The same holds true today. Always inquire of the Counsel of the LORD before you go to war. Ask the LORD to show you how to pray to overcome the spiritual forces opposing your restoration.

Elisha asked the LORD to open the eyes of his servant so he could see that there were more hosts of heaven fighting for them than there were hosts of enemies against them.[183] As you pray, ask the LORD to give you eyes of faith to "see" like the servant of Elisha so you can know that there are many more spiritual hosts fighting for you than against you.

When I battle, I often use two names of God: The Ancient of Days and Yahweh. I call on the Ancient of Days as the Sovereign Ruler of the Universe, the Judge of all men who has ruled in favor of the saints in order that we may possess the Kingdom of God.[184] I also call on the Great I AM, Yahweh, the covenant-keeping, covenant-fulfilling name of God. I encourage you to meditate on the names of God and use them as you fast, pray and obtain victory over the unseen enemies assigned to oppose your restoration. The Word of God is your sword and is backed by the covenant name of God.

---

183. 2 Kings 6:17

184. Daniel 7:22

Therefore God also has highly exalted Him and given Him the name which is above every name,

That at the name of Jesus every knee should bow, of those in heaven and of those on earth and of those under the earth,

And that every tongue should confess that Jesus Christ is Lord, to the glory of God the Father.

—PHILIPPIANS 2:9-11

When I pray, I issue decrees from the Word of God and decree the sending out of arrows, the ends of which have the covenant oaths or covenant promises of God on them. In Habakkuk, the prophet appeals in prayer to God to work on behalf of the people of Israel:

O LORD, I have heard Your speech and was afraid; O LORD, revive Your work in the midst of the years! In the midst of the years make it known; In wrath remember mercy.

God came from Teman, the Holy One from Mount Paran. Selah. His glory covered the heavens, and the earth was full of His praise.

His brightness was like the light; He had rays flashing from His hand, and there His power was hidden.

Before Him went pestilence, and fever followed at His feet.

He stood and measured the earth; He looked and startled the nations. And the everlasting mountains were scattered, the perpetual hills bowed. His ways are everlasting.

I saw the tents of Cushan in affliction; the curtains of the land of Midian trembled.

O LORD, were you displeased with the rivers, was Your anger against the rivers, was Your wrath against the sea, that you rode on Your horses, Your chariots of salvation?

Your bow was made quite ready; Oaths were sworn over Your *arrows*. Selah

—HABAKKUK 3:1-9

The word "arrows" in Habakkuk 3:9 is the Hebrew word *matteh* often used for the tribes of Israel, but in this instance means spear:

Thy bow was made bare, the rods of chastisement were sworn.

—HABAKKUK 3:9 NASB

The word for "bare" is the Hebrew word *eryah* which means a naked or bare bow, metaphorically used to indicate the outpouring of God's wrath on Earth by God's bow being naked or uncovered, meaning it was taken out of hiding and is now to be put into use in battle. The word for "rods" is the Hebrew word *matteh* and means a rod or staff, but in this instance, it means a spear used in battle. The word for "sworn" is the Hebrew word *shbuwah* and means an oath or sacred promise like the oath God made to Abraham, Isaac and Jacob that He would fulfill His covenant to them and their seed.

When I use this Scripture in battle, I decree God's covenant promises and oaths of restoration. These oaths are immutable and unchangeable and are placed on the end of the spiritual arrows that are sent out to pierce the unseen enemy.

In this prayer, the prophet Habakkuk appeals to the LORD to remember the deliverance He performed years prior when Israel was coming out of Egypt and going through the wilderness to the land of promise. The prophet reminds the LORD how He miraculously intervened in assisting Israel in battle and appeals to the LORD in covenant mercy to once again bring a miraculous deliverance by "reviving Your work in the midst of the years!"

Here is a prayer you might want to consider:

PRAYER

Father, I call on You, the Ancient of Days, the Sovereign of the Universe, the Judge of all men and the Just Judge of all Earth. You have ruled in favor of Your saints to possess the Kingdom of God, so I now go in to possess my inheritance of restoration. I call on the Great I AM, *Yahweh*, the covenant-keeping God, who keeps His covenant of mercy to a thousand generations to those who love You.

I call on the hosts of heaven to establish Your covenant restoration over my life. I decree oaths from Your promises of restoration found in Your Word over arrows I send out to scatter the unseen foes in my life, lightning in abundance to vanquish the enemy opposed to my intended restoration.

I decree that the plans of the enemy which have sought to hinder my intended restoration are nullified, foiled and brought to nothing. I decree Your Counsel stands over my life.

AMEN

Restoration comes through the Spirit of grace working in and through our circumstances. The prophet Zechariah states,

This is the word of the LORD to Zerubbabel: "Not by might nor by power, but by My Spirit," says the LORD of hosts.

"Who are you, O great mountain? Before Zerubbabel you shall become a plain! And he shall bring forth the capstone with shouts of 'Grace, grace to it!'"

—ZECHARIAH 4:6

Zechariah was speaking to Zerubbabel, the governor of Judah, who was responsible for the rebuilding of the post-exilic temple. Zechariah declared that neither might, nor the resources of man would restore the temple of God, but rather, the temple's restoration would be accomplished by the Spirit of God.

The mountain referred to by Zechariah in this Scripture was a metaphor for every obstruction and opposition in the way of the temple's building plans. Zechariah said to Zerubbabel that any obstruction and opposition in the way of the building plans would come down, not through the law and not through human strength, but solely through shouts of "Grace, grace!"

Before David became king of Israel, he stood in battle against the Philistine giant Goliath. David said to Goliath,

"You come to me with a sword, with a spear and with a javelin. But I come to you in the name of the LORD of hosts, the God of the armies of Israel, whom you have defied.

"This day the LORD will deliver you into my hand, and I will strike you and take your head from you. And this day I will give the carcasses of the camp of the Philistines to the birds of the air and the wild beasts of the earth, that all the earth may know that there is a God in Israel.

"Then all this assembly shall know that the LORD does not save with sword and spear; for the battle is the LORD's and He will give you into our hands."

—1 SAMUEL 17:45-47

David had previously rejected wearing King Saul's metal armament and had rejected using his sword for the battle. Instead, David chose five smooth stones and put them in a shepherd's bag. David then took one of the stones and slung it. True to its mark, the stone hit Goliath in his forehead and killed him.[185]

David rejected the traditional and earthly weapons of war, the sword and spear, representing the strength of man or the strength of the flesh. Instead, David chose five smooth stones, five representing the number of grace. Notice that the stones were smooth, representing the ease of grace. Notice that the stones were carried in a shepherd's bag, a humble place where grace is found. And finally, notice that it only took one smooth stone, through the Spirit's power, to make this giant Philistine mountain become a plain.

Do you have a giant mountain in your way of restoration? Begin declaring "Grace, grace" over it. Are there hindrances and barriers in your way of restoration? Declare that the hindrances become a plain and submit to shouts of "Grace, grace." Ask the Spirit of grace, God's Holy Spirit, to penetrate your circumstances and take them over.

Make sure you are not "fighting" the spiritual opposition in your flesh. Rather, let God remove the mountains by His Spirit. Through a direct and decisive commitment to fast and offer Spirit-led prayer, welcome in the power and provision of the Spirit of grace. Remember, the battle is the LORD's, but He has promised to remove the mountain by and through His Spirit with shouts of "Grace, grace!"

---

185. 1 Samuel 17:38-49

ℛESTORATION REQUIRES COVENANT

℟ estoration requires covenant with God. God is the covenant initiator and He is the covenant fulfiller.

The word "covenant" is the Hebrew word *briyth*, which means contract, treaty, pact or agreement. The word is first used in Scripture when God made a covenant with Noah. He said:

> And for Me, behold, I establish My covenant with you and with your descendants after you,
>
> And with every living creature that is with you: the birds, the cattle and every beast of the earth with you, of all that go out of the ark, every beast of the earth.
>
> Thus I establish My covenant with you: Never again shall all flesh be cut off by the waters of the flood; never again shall there be a flood to destroy the earth."

And God said: "This is the sign of the covenant which I make between Me and you, and every living creature that is with you, for perpetual generations:

I set My rainbow in the cloud, and it shall be for the sign of the covenant between Me and the earth.

It shall be, when I bring a cloud over the earth, that the rainbow shall be seen in the cloud;

And I will remember My covenant which is between Me and you and every living creature of all flesh; the waters shall never again become a flood to destroy all flesh.

The rainbow shall be in the cloud, and I will look on it to remember the everlasting covenant between God and every living creature of all flesh that is on the earth."

And God said to Noah, "This is the sign of the covenant which I have established between Me and all flesh that is on the earth."

—GENESIS 9:9-17

The covenant with Noah is the first covenant made by God, and it was made to man and to every living thing that God had created. In this covenant, God promised He would never again bring a flood to destroy the earth.

The second covenant made by God was with Abram.[186] This covenant was affirmed by God thirteen years later when He states,

And I will make My covenant between Me and you, and will multiply you exceedingly.[187]

---

186. Genesis 15
187. Genesis 17:1-10

As for Me, behold, My covenant is with you, and you shall be a father of many nations.

—GENESIS 17:2,4

And I will establish My covenant between me and you and your descendants after you in their generations, for an everlasting covenant, to be God to you and your descendants after you.

—GENESIS 17:7

God irrevocably pledges to be God to Abram (later named "Abraham") and his descendants forever. Contrary to the covenant God made with Noah that included all of mankind and every living creature, God's covenant with Abraham was solely with Abraham and his descendants.

After He made the covenant with Abraham, God required blood to become a sign of the covenant:

This is My covenant which you shall keep, between Me and you and your descendants after you: Every male child among you shall be circumcised;

And you shall be circumcised in the flesh of your foreskins, and it shall be a sign of the covenant between Me and you.

He who is eight days old among you shall be circumcised, every male child in your generations, he who is born in your house or bought with money from any foreigner who is not your descendant.

He who is born in your house and he who is bought with your money must be circumcised and My covenant shall be in your flesh for an everlasting covenant.

—GENESIS 17:10-13

As a sign of the covenant, God required the foreskin of the flesh of the male reproductive organ to be cut away. This act symbolized a cutting away of depending on the arm of flesh that brings a curse as opposed to depending on God through faith that brings a blessing.[188]

After Abraham, God made a covenant with the nation of Israel. The covenant was based on the law of God written by God on tablets called the Ten Commandments. Moses, God's leader to the nation, prophet and spokesman, brought God's law to the nation and the people received the law saying, "All that the LORD has spoken we will do."[189]

From this declaration, a covenant relationship between God and the nation was formed.

After the covenant was formed, an altar was built, sacrifices were made and blood (representing confirmation of the covenant) was sprinkled on the altar, on the people and on the Book of the Covenant.7 Moses then said, "This is the blood of the covenant which the LORD has made with you according to all these words."[190]

As time went on, the nation failed to honor the covenant and as a result, the nation went into exile and captivity and was plundered by the surrounding nations.

Wherever there is captivity, exile, loss, plundering and separation, there is a broken covenant with God. When an individual or nation experiences captivity, loss and plundering, you find an individual or nation that has departed from and broken covenant with God. Broken covenant leads to captivity, exile, loss and separation.

---

188. Jeremiah 17:5-8

189. Exodus 19:8

190. Exodus 24:8

When God made His covenant with the nation, He called heaven and Earth as a witness to the binding of the covenant relationship:

> Take heed to yourselves, lest you forget the covenant of the LORD your God which He made with you, and make for yourselves a carved image in the form of anything which the LORD your God has forbidden you.
>
> For the LORD your God is a consuming fire, a jealous God.
>
> I call heaven and earth to witness against you this day, that you will soon utterly perish from the land which you cross over the Jordan to possess; you will not prolong your days in it, but will be utterly destroyed.
>
> —DEUTERONOMY 4:23-24, 26

> "I call heaven and earth as witnesses today against you, that I have set before you life and death, blessing and cursing; therefore choose life, that both you and your descendants may live;
>
> That you may love the LORD your God, that you may obey His voice, and that you may cling to Him, for He is your life and the length of your days; and that you may dwell in the land which the LORD swore to your fathers, to Abraham, Isaac and Jacob to give them."
>
> —DEUTERONOMY 30:19-20

God's covenant with Israel was both spiritual and natural. God called the heavens (spiritual) and Earth (natural) as witnesses to the covenant. God and the nation were now bound in covenant before heaven and Earth, and heaven and Earth became a witness to the covenant—blessings of life and peace if obedient to the covenant, and the curse of death and destruction if disobedient to the covenant.

The concept of heaven and Earth becoming witnesses to obedience to the law of God and the keeping of covenant is of profound legal and spiritual significance. Covenant with God produces a witness in the heavens and a witness on Earth; a witness in favor of us when we obey God and a witness against us when we disobey God.

Obedience or disobedience will determine whether we will be recipients of blessings or curses in both the spiritual and natural realms of our lives and circumstances. Obedience brings spiritual and natural blessings (unity with God, life, length of days, dwelling and prospering in the land) and disobedience brings spiritual and natural curses (separation from God, loss, plundering, exile and a separation His blessings).

A NEW COVENANT

God tells us that although a broken covenant leads to captivity and death, returning to the terms of the covenant leads to life and peace—Divine Restoration. God declared through the prophet Jeremiah that God would make a *new covenant* with the house of Israel and the house of Judah:

> "Behold the days are coming," says the LORD, "when I will make a new covenant with the house of Israel and with the house of Judah—

> "Not according to the covenant that I made with their fathers in the day that I took them by the hand to lead them out of the land of Egypt, My covenant which they broke, though I was a husband to them," says the LORD.

> "But this is the covenant that I will make with the house of Israel after those days," says the LORD: "I will put My law in

their minds, and write it on their hearts; and I will be their God, and they shall be My people."

—JEREMIAH 31:31-33

The new covenant cited in Jeremiah 31:31-33 is the covenant brought to life in men's hearts by grace through faith in the Son of God, Jesus Christ. During the Passover feast in Jerusalem, just before Jesus Christ became the Passover Lamb of God "who takes away the sins of the world," Jesus met with His disciples to have their last Passover meal.[191] In Luke 22:19-20 there is an account of the Passover meal. In this account, Jesus took bread, gave thanks, broke it and gave it to His disciples and said, "This is My body which is given for you, do this in remembrance of Me." Likewise, He also took the cup after supper saying, "This cup is the new covenant in My blood, which is shed for you."

The word "covenant" used in Luke 22:19-20 is the Greek word *diatheke* and means will, testament or pact. Jesus Christ declared before His disciples and before heaven and Earth that His death on the cross would become the new covenant that God would now offer to all of mankind.

The Apostle Paul terms it a "better covenant" because it is based on better promises. The promises are better because the promises are based on the unmerited favor God freely bestowed on man, through the grace of Jesus Christ, the *mediator* of the new covenant.[192] The word "mediator" used in Hebrews 12:24 is the Greek word *mesites* and means a go-between, a reconciler or one who intervenes between. Jesus Christ became the mediator and reconciler of the new covenant that

---

191. Luke 22:7-16

192. Hebrews 7:22, 8:6, 12:24

was now eternally offered between God and man. This new covenant is individually accessed and received into our lives by receiving forgiveness for breaking covenant with God. Our forgiveness is offered by grace through faith in Jesus Christ.

In Titus 3:5 the Apostle Paul reminds us that by the kindness and the love of God, not by works of righteousness which we have done, but according to God's mercy, He saved us through the washing of regeneration and renewing of the Holy Spirit. Paul also explains in Philippians 3:9 that he counts all things in his life as rubbish so that he may gain Christ and be found in Him, "not having my own righteousness, which is from the law, but that which is through faith in Christ, the righteousness which is from God by faith. ."

God is seeking from us a covenant relationship with Him like He had with Abraham, a covenant relationship based on faith. Abraham was called a friend of God.[193] The Apostle James writes,

> And the Scripture was fulfilled which says, "Abraham believed God, and it was accounted to him for righteousness." And he was called the friend of God.
>
> —JAMES 2:23

The word "friend" used in James 2:23 is the Greek word *philos* and means loved one, beloved and affectionate friend. This is what God wants us to become to Him—an affectionate friend, a friendship based on mutuality and love.

Jesus Christ uses this same word for *friend* when He declared that if we will do what He commands, we will be called His friends:

---

193. 2 Chronicles 20:7

You are my friends if you do whatever I command you. No longer do I call you servants, for a servant does not know what his master is doing; but I have called you friends, for all things that I heard from My Father I have made known to you.

—JOHN 15:14-15

When we open our hearts to Jesus Christ and place our faith in Jesus Christ for eternal life, we become children of God, heirs of God through Christ.[194] If we are heirs of God through Christ, then we also become spiritual seeds (heirs) of Abraham and heirs to the promises God gave to Abraham according to the covenant God made with him.[195]

Romans 4:3 states that Abraham believed God, and it was accounted to Him for righteousness. In this verse, the word "believed" is the Greek word *pisteuo,* which means to be persuaded firmly as to something with hope of a certain expectation. God gave Abraham a promise that he would be a father of many nations and that he would have a son, even though Abraham and his wife Sarah were well past the age of childbearing.[196] Although all natural circumstances were contrary to the fulfillment of this promise, Abraham was fully persuaded, and, contrary to hope, *in hope he believed.*[197]

God is looking for a covenant relationship with us that produces covenant faith, faith like Abraham, a friend of God. As an heir of Abraham through faith in Jesus Christ, we are entitled to every promise of blessing and restoration found in the Word of God. However, the

---

194. Galatians 3:29, 4:1-7

195. Ibid

196. Genesis 18:10-11

197. Romans 4:18

promise of blessings and restoration must be received and acted on through the righteousness of faith:

> He (Abraham) did not waver at the promise of God through unbelief, but was strengthened in faith, giving glory to God,
>
> And being fully convinced that what He had promised He was also able to perform.
>
> And therefore "it was accounted to him for righteousness."
>
> —ROMANS 4:20-22

COVENANT FAITH

Abraham had covenant faith in God. Covenant faith is active, not passive. It is *believing* God contrary to natural circumstances and not wavering on the promise no matter how impossible the fulfillment of the promise may seem. It is believing there is nothing too hard for the LORD. Covenant faith partners with God to witness the natural circumstances line up with the LORD's promises.

The Greek word used for the phrase "fully convinced" in Romans 4:21 is the word *plerophoreo* and means completely assured or fully persuaded. In other words, Abraham did not need any additional assurances or evidence from God to believe and to act by faith on God's Word to him. Abraham was completely assured and fully persuaded.

The LORD seeks covenant faith from each one of His children. Covenant faith ushers in Divine Restoration.

As you pursue an Isaiah 58 fast, ask yourself some questions:

- Am I in covenant with God?

- Have I broken covenant with God and need to return to Him?

- Do I have a true and sincere pact and testament with God based on the blood of God's only Son, Jesus Christ?

- Am I fully convinced of God's promises in my life for my restoration?

- Do I need more evidence that God's desires and fully supports a full restoration for me, my family and nation?

- Am I like Abraham who was fully persuaded of the promise made by God to him *and,* therefore, acted in obedient faith to all that God asked him to do?

- Am I completely assured and fully persuaded, or do I need more convincing?

- Am I acting in faith and doing all that God has asked me to do?

- Am I wavering and double minded?

If you don't know where you stand on the pendulum of faith, ask the LORD to reveal any wavering in your faith. Ask the LORD to not only to increase your faith, but also to establish and anchor your faith in Him and His Word. The Apostles who walked with Jesus Christ in the flesh for three years had to ask God to increase their faith.[198] There is no sin in asking God to increase your faith. NOT to ask God to increase your faith and fail to receive God's promised restoration because of unbelief would be sin. Ask and keep asking until you receive the covenant faith you need for pursuing restoration in your life. A Scripture that SHOUTS victory and encourages faith declares,

---

198. Luke 17:5

For whatever is born of God overcomes the world. And this is the victory that has overcome the world-our faith.

—1 JOHN 5:4

Covenant faith is what overcomes the world and all the destructive circumstances the world has thrown at you. Be not dismayed. The Scripture emphatically declares that you overcome the world through faith.

Covenant faith is a weighty topic, the depths and riches of which cannot be fully explored here or in any one book. In simple terms, covenant faith is found in one who is fully convinced of God's goodness and fully convinced of God's promises and, therefore, obeys God in all things. Covenant faith is the Counsel of the LORD for your life.

The Apostle Peter's life is a great example of a person who began by having a covenant relationship with God and after his denial of God came to understand and have covenant faith in God. The Apostle had the incredible privilege to walk with Jesus Christ in a personal, living and dynamic relationship on Earth. However, the LORD told Peter that he would deny Him when the time came for the LORD to be judged and crucified:

Then He said, "I tell you, Peter, the rooster shall not crow this day before you will deny three times that you know Me."

—LUKE 22:34

However, the LORD knew that one day, shortly after Peter's faith was tried and sifted, that Peter would return and fulfill the Counsel of God in his life—to "strengthen your brethren."[199]

199. Luke 22:31-32

At the time of Peter's denial, he was in a covenant relationship with God and knew that Jesus was the Christ, the Son of the living God.[200] Although Peter had a covenant relationship with God, he was not yet in a place of covenant faith in God, a place of being fully convinced and fully persuaded, a place of unwavering faith.

After Jesus Christ was crucified and raised from the dead, Jesus came to Peter and the other disciples by the Sea of Tiberias. It was at this time that Christ wanted to meet with Peter, face-to-face. Christ wanted to offer Peter a chance to embrace unwavering, fully convinced, covenant faith:

> After these things Jesus showed Himself again to the disciples at the Sea of Tiberias, and in this way He showed Himself:
>
> Simon Peter, Thomas called the Twin, Nathanael of Cana in Galilee, the sons of Zebedee, and two others of His disciples were together.
>
> Simon Peter said to them, "I am going fishing."
>
> They said to him, "We are going with you also." They went out and immediately got into the boat, and that night they caught nothing.
>
> But when the morning had now come, Jesus stood on the shore; yet the disciples did not know that it was Jesus.
>
> Then Jesus said to them, "Children, have you any food?" They answered Him, "No."
>
> And He said to them, "Cast the net on the right side of the boat, and you will find some." So they cast, and now they were not able to draw it in because of the multitude of fish.

200. Matthew 16:13-20

Therefore that disciple whom Jesus loved said to Peter, "it is the Lord!" Now when Simon Peter heard that it was the Lord, he put on his outer garment (for he had removed it) and plunged into the sea.

—JOHN 21:1-7

So when they had eaten breakfast, Jesus said to Simon Peter, "Simon, son of Jonah, do you love Me more than these?"

He said to Him, "Yes, Lord; You know that I love you." He said to him, "Feed My lambs."

He said to him again a second time, "Simon, son of Jonah, do you love Me?"

He said to Him, "Yes, Lord: You know that I love You."

He said to him, "Tend My sheep."

He said to him the third time, "Simon, son of Jonah, do you love Me?"

Peter was grieved because He said to him the third time, "Do you love Me?"

And he said to Him," Lord, You know all things: You know that I love You."

Jesus said to him, "Feed My sheep."

—JOHN 21:15-17

In this account, Jesus Christ gently encounters His greatly beloved disciple and restores him through a series of probing questions, questions related to matters of the heart. Jesus asks Peter three times, "Do you love Me?" After Peter had the opportunity to accept Christ's invitation of restoration, Jesus reiterates to Peter his original calling from God, "Feed My sheep."

It is after this encounter with the risen LORD that Peter, a man who had a covenant relationship with the LORD, became a man who now manifested covenant faith in the LORD. In fact, the greatest accounts of the Apostle Peter's life are found *after* Peter was restored to embrace a life of covenant faith.[201]

The way Christ came to Peter is how Christ comes to each one of us today—by asking us, "Do you love Me?" The LORD wants to give to each one of us covenant faith in Him, a covenant faith based on true and sincere, unwavering, and unshakable love—God's love. This covenant love is what unwavering faith is based on. Covenant love makes us bold and causes us to have an unwavering faith in God. This type of love is available only through the risen LORD.

The Scripture says,

> And we have known and believed the love that God has for us. God is love, and he who abides in love abides in God, and God in him.
>
> Love has been perfected among us in this: that we may have boldness in the day of judgment; because as He is, so are we in this world.
>
> There is no fear in love; but perfect love casts out fear, because fear involves torment. But he who fears has not been made perfect in love.
>
> —1 JOHN 4:16-18

201. Acts 2-5, 12, 15

In perfect love, covenant faith is born, maintained and perfected. Ask yourself some questions:

- Am I like Peter, have I walked away from the Lord through fear?

- Have I set aside *covenant faith* (even though I have a covenant relationship with God) because of some disappointment or circumstances that shook my faith and caused me to fear?

No doubt, the LORD wants to jumpstart in you covenant faith in Him. Now is the time to set aside fear, disappointments and past circumstances that tested and tried your faith. It is time to become like the Apostle Peter and "plunge into the sea, swim back to the shore and meet the risen LORD." It is there the LORD will meet you and ask you, "Do you love Me?" And it is there the LORD will direct you back to your original calling to "feed His sheep."

Now is the time to return to your first love. Now is the time to return to a covenant with God. In God's covenant love you will have covenant faith to feed the LORD's sheep. In feeding the LORD's sheep— the individuals placed in your life— you will find your restoration. Covenant love plus covenant faith equals covenant restoration. This is the Divine Restoration plan for you, your family and nation.

God promised to return to Zion and dwell in Jerusalem.[202] In Zechariah 8:7, God promised to bring back His people whom He had scattered throughout the earth because of rebellion. Once the remnant of the nation returned to God, God declared that He would reverse the negative conditions they had suffered. He declared,

---

202. Zechariah 8

"But now I will not treat the remnant of this people as in the former days," says the LORD of hosts.

"For the seed shall be prosperous, the vine shall give it's fruit, the ground shall give her increase, and the heavens shall give their dew—I will cause the remnant of this people to possess all these.

"And it shall come to pass that just as you were a curse among the nations, O house of Judah and house of Israel, so I will save you, and you shall be a blessing, do not fear, let your hands be strong."

For thus says the LORD of hosts: "Just as I determined to punish you when your fathers provoked Me to wrath," says the LORD of hosts, "and I would not relent, so again in these days I am determined to do good to Jerusalem and to the house of Judah. Do not fear.

"These are the things you shall do; Speak each man the truth to his neighbor; give judgment in your gates for truth, justice and peace;

"Let none of you think evil in your heart against your neighbor; and do not love a false oath. For all these are things that I hate," says the LORD.

—ZECHARIAH 8:11-17

The promise of restoration given through the prophet Zechariah is for all of us if we will return to God in covenant faith. God promises to "do good" to us, to cause our seed to be prosperous, to cause our vine to give its' fruit, to cause our ground to increase and to cause the heavens to give their dew. And the LORD promises to help us to possess these promises. But possession of these promises only comes through covenant faith.

Decide today to join the LORD in covenant faith. Take your hand out of your pocket, take your hand from behind your back and reach out your hand to the LORD today. His hand has been stretched out to you, and now it is time for you to take His hand and let His covenant love flow to you like a never ending stream of mercy—to your heart, to your mind, to your body and into your life for *Divine Restoration*.

This is the plan of the LORD for you. You are the Bride of Christ and the LORD is your Bridegroom. In this covenant union is found the fullness of your *Divine Restoration*. Join your Bridegroom today in covenant faith, don't delay.

ℛESTORATION REQUIRES PARDON

estoration requires you to receive and accept a pardon from the LORD. Pardon is a spiritually significant word. In the Scriptures, the word "pardon" comes from the Hebrew word *salach* and means to forgive, spare someone or to relieve someone of the burden of their offense. It is a verb, the only subject of which is God, for He is the only person who has the power and authority to pardon sin.[203] When God pardons sin, it is as if the sin never happened. In other words, when God pardons, He not only relieves the penalty or punishment for the offense, but also removes from His mind the memory of the offense.[204]

Consider for a moment the power of this statement, "God removes from His mind the memory of the sin, as if it never happened." The

---

203. Psalm 103:3, Luke 5:21-24

204. Psalm 103:12

fact that God does not remember sin once it has been pardoned is an astounding fact.

Is it possible to live out the reality of never remembering past sins nor remembering the sins of others? The answer is YES! It is possible. However, pardon must be desired and received with all your heart.

Experience the power of pardon found in Psalm 103:

> Bless the LORD, O my soul; and all that is within me, bless His holy name!
>
> Bless the LORD, O my soul, and forget not all His benefits:
>
> Who *forgives* (pardons) all your *iniquities*, who heals all your diseases,
>
> Who redeems your life from destruction, who crowns you with lovingkindness and tender mercies,
>
> Who satisfied your mouth with good things, so that your youth is renewed like the eagle's.
>
> The LORD executes righteousness and justice for all who are oppressed.
>
> He made known His ways to Moses, and His acts to the children of Israel.
>
> The LORD is merciful and gracious, slow to anger and abounding in mercy.
>
> He will not always strive with us, nor will He keep His anger forever.
>
> He has not dealt with us according to our sins, nor punished us according to our iniquities.

For as the heavens are high above the earth, so great is His mercy toward those who fear Him;

As far as the east is from the west, so far as He removed our transgressions from us.

As a father pities his children, so the LORD pities those who fear Him.

For He knows our frame; He remembers that we are dust.

As for a man, his days are like grass; as a flower of the field, so he flourishes.

For the wind passes over it, and it is gone, and its place remembers it no more.

But the mercy of the LORD is from everlasting to everlasting on those who fear Him, and His righteousness to children's children,

To such as keep His covenant, and to those who remember His commandments to do them.

The LORD has established His throne in heaven, and His kingdom rules over all.

Bless the LORD, you His angels, who excel in strength and who do His word, heeding the voice of His word.

Bless the LORD, all you His hosts, you ministers of His, who do His pleasure.

Bless the LORD, all His works, in all places of His dominion. Bless the LORD, O my soul!

—PSALM 103

Inspired of God, King David wrote this Psalm. It declares that God is the one Who forgives (*salach*—pardons, spares, relieves someone of the burden of an offense) all our iniquities. The word "iniquity" is the Hebrew word *avown* and means evil or guilt and carries with it the idea of deliberately twisting or perverting. It is the same word that Isaiah uses when he declares the reason God's hand is unable to bring healing and restoration to the nation:

> Behold, the LORD's hand is not shortened, that it cannot save, nor His ear heavy that it cannot hear.
>
> But your iniquities have separated you from your God; and your sins have hidden His face from you, so that He will not hear.
>
> —ISAIAH 59:1-2

Not only does God forgive and pardon our twisting and perverting of His Law, but also He removes our transgression from us as "far as the east is from the west."[205] The word "transgression" used by King David is the Hebrew word *pasha* and means rebellion or to rebel, revolt or trespass. It carries with it the meaning to break out against.

This word is also used by Isaiah when he cited the sins of the nation, the product of which produced a web of lies that covered the nation and the people:

> For our transgressions are multiplied before You, and our sins testify against us. For our transgressions are with us, and as for our iniquities, we know them:

205. Ibid

In transgressing and lying against the LORD, and departing from our God, speaking oppression and revolt, conceiving and uttering from the heart words of falsehood.

Justice is turned back, and righteousness stands afar off; for truth is fallen in the street, and equity cannot enter.

So truth fails, and he who departs from evil makes himself a prey.

—ISAIAH 59:12-15

God promises to pardon our transgression against Him and to remove its remembrance.[206] This is the sum and substance of a pardon—a removal of sin and its effect *"as far as the east is from the west."*

While writing this chapter, the Lord gave me a vision. In the vision on the left was the presence of sin, its vileness and burden of bondage. Then, from the right side came what appeared to be a tidal wave of the blood of Jesus Christ. Once the title wave of the blood of Jesus Christ was released, it washed away the sin and its vileness, its weight, burden and effect. Sin and its consequences were removed as if the sin had never been there before.

A pardon from God entails a wiping away of sin as if it never existed. A pardon can be likened to going to the beach and writing in the sand all of the sins you have ever committed, everything you have ever done, everything you have ever thought and everything you have ever said that was against God. Once you are finished writing in the sand, a wave from the ocean comes to the shore and washes over every single word you wrote in the sand. Once the wave moves back into the sea, everything you wrote in the sand has been erased and washed away. All that is left is the pure, untouched sandy shoreline. What does a pardon

---

206. Ibid

from God look like: a washing away or removal of sin, as if it never happened?

God shows us how He issues a pardon when He encounters the religious leaders of His day who were called to apply and administer the Law to a woman caught in the sin of adultery:

> Now early in the morning He came again into the temple, and all the people came to Him; and He sat down and taught them.
>
> Then the scribes and Pharisees brought to Him a woman caught in adultery.
>
> And when they had set her in the midst, they said to Him, "Teacher, this woman was caught in adultery, in the very act.
>
> "Now Moses, in the law, commanded us that such should be stoned. But what do you say?"
>
> This they said, testing Him, that they might have something of which to accuse Him. But Jesus stooped down and wrote on the ground with His finger, as though He did not hear.
>
> So when they continued asking Him, He raised Himself up and said to them, "He who is without sin among you, let him throw a stone at her first."
>
> And again He stooped down and wrote on the ground.
>
> Then those who heard it, being convicted by their conscience, went out one by one, beginning with the oldest even to the last. And Jesus was left alone, and the woman standing in the midst.
>
> When Jesus had raised Himself up and saw no one but the woman, He said to her, "Woman, where are those accusers of yours? Has no one condemned you?"
>
> She said, "No one, Lord."

And Jesus said to her, "*Neither do I condemn you; go and sin no more.*"

Then Jesus spoke to them again saying, "I am the light of the world. He who follows Me shall not walk in darkness, but have the light of life."

—JOHN 8:2-12

In the Law of Moses, if a person were caught in the act of adultery, that person was to be stoned.[207] God, however, offered this woman a pardon under the new covenant law of grace and truth. The Judge of the Universe did not issue the death penalty under the Law of Moses, but rather a judgment of life, a full pardon, under the new covenant law of grace. A profound legal and spiritual transaction took place in the temple that day. The Judge of all men issued His divine and righteous verdict to a woman guilty of the sin deserving of death and declared, "Neither do I *condemn* you. Go and sin no more."[208]

The Greek word for the word "condemn" in John 8 is the word *katakrino* and means to judge or to pronounce a sentence upon. In issuing His righteous verdict, God declared, "I am neither judging you, nor pronouncing a sentence against you for this offence, but now, *go and sin no more.*"

GOD'S PARDON

When the LORD began speaking to me about the word *pardon*, He asked me to begin praying for a pardon for others. In doing so, I began to research this word and found that I had not fully understood the depth of the LORD's pardon.

---

207. Leviticus 20:10

208. John 8:11

As I began my quest, God recalled to my mind an individual who had shared her life story involving a sordid and crooked past. When she came to mind, God took me in the Spirit realm to a place where I had absolutely no recollection of the details of her past. In fact, for that moment, as hard as I tried to remember, I could not remember a single word she had told me about her sin-filled life. In that moment, God allowed me to experience how He handles pardons—He removes the offense and *has no memory of it*. Then, the LORD began to explain the contrast between the way He handles pardons and the way we have been handling pardons. The two are not the same.

To understand how we have been receiving and issuing pardons in contrast to the way God issues a pardon, I considered how pardons are issued in my home state. My home state has several types of pardons: a full pardon, a conditional pardon, and a pardon based on innocence. A full pardon releases you from the conditions of your sentence, restores basic rights to you (right to vote, right to serve on a jury, and so forth) and restores some but not all barriers to employment and professional licensing.

A conditional pardon is like a full pardon except it does not restore any rights you lost as a result of the conviction. A pardon based on innocence, however, not only pardons you for the crime and releases you from further punishment, but also declares you innocent and erases the conviction. In order to receive this type of exoneration, you must prove innocence from at least two trial officials or through a finding by a judge.

We all have bought the lie of living in a state of a "conditional pardon" rather than living in a state of a "pardon for innocence." We often not only deny ourselves the right to a pardon for innocence, but we deny others this right as well. All the while, God has issued to us a full, unconditional pardon of innocence, restoring very right and spiritual benefit back to us as His sons and daughters, not remembering our sins and removing them *"as far as the east is from the west."*

If God, who is righteous, has declared that a pardon for innocence can be found through the blood atonement of His Son, Jesus Christ, then who are we to deny the LORD Jesus Christ by failing to receive or to give a pardon based on innocence? Who are we to sit as judge and jury and condemn ourselves by not receiving a full pardon? Who are we to issue a conditional pardon to others when God has issued a pardon based on innocence to us? Are we greater and more just than God?

While I was studying the meaning of a pardon, the LORD gave a vision of a vial of blood. I asked the LORD, "What is this?"

The LORD then asked me, "What does a person do with a vial of blood?"

"Take it to have it examined and tested to see what is in the blood," I replied.

"Exactly. I want you to start examining and testing *My* blood to find out what I AM really made of," He answered.

The truth of the matter is that we have all failed to learn what the LORD is really made of, who HE really IS. But the time of ignorance is at an end. God wants us to find out what HE IS really made of. A pardon for innocence is what the divine blood of Jesus Christ gave to us when He died on a Roman cross and triumphantly rose from the grave. Jesus Christ destroyed the curse of sin that kept us from receiving a pardon for innocence.

Receiving for yourself and issuing to others a pardon for innocence is essential for restoration. Make a decisive decision to pursue a pardon for yourself and with each person the Holy Spirit recalls to mind. Issue a pardon for innocence to yourself and the other person. Begin this process by receiving a pardon for yourself and for those who have hurt you the most or caused you the greatest pain. Seek you pardon and then their pardon. You cannot give what you have not first received.

We are commanded to love our enemies, do good to those who hate us and to pray for those who spitefully use us, for through this act of faith and obedience we become complete in maturity and like our Father in heaven:

> You have heard that it was said, "You shall love your neighbor and hate your enemy."
>
> But I say to you, "Love your enemies, bless those who curse you, do good to those who hate you, and pray for those who spitefully use you and persecute you,
>
> "That you may be sons of your Father in heaven; for He makes His sun rise on the evil and on the good, and sends rain on the just and on the unjust.
>
> "For if you love those who love you, what reward have you? Do not even the tax collectors do the same?
>
> "And if you greet your brethren only, what do you do more than others? Do not even the tax collectors do so?
>
> "Therefore you shall be perfect, just as your Father in heaven is perfect."
>
> —MATTHEW 5:43-48

The book of Job declares how God restored Job's losses, double and tells of the end of his life.[209] Before the LORD issued a double portion return, Job was required to pray for his friends who had not spoken kindly or rightly to Job about God:

> And so it was, after the LORD had spoken these words to Job, that the LORD said to Eliphaz the Temanite, "My wrath

---

209. Job 42:10

is aroused against you and your two friends, for you have not spoken of Me what is right as My servant Job has.

"Now therefore, take for yourselves seven bulls and seven rams, go to My servant Job, and offer up for yourselves a burnt offering; and My servant Job shall pray for you. For I will accept him, lest I deal with you according to your folly; because you have not spoken of Me what is right, as My servant Job has."

So Eliphaz the Temanite and Bildad the Shuhite and Zophar the Naamathite went and did as the LORD commanded them; for the LORD had accepted Job.

And the LORD restored Job's losses when he prayed for his friends. Indeed the LORD gave Job twice as much as he had before.

—JOB 42:7-10

The word "prayed" in this verse is the Hebrew word *palal* and means to entreat and intercede on behalf of someone. When Job entreated God to forgive his friends, God turned the captivity of Job and restored to Job a double portion of all he had lost. Restoration of all that Job had lost occurred after Job prayed for the pardon of his friends.

Praying for the pardon of individuals who have hurt you or caused injuries in your life is essential to restoration. You simply cannot move forward and go into your good future without sincerely pardoning yourself and others. Issuing a pardon is the LORD's Counsel and a spiritual mandate for restoration.

Judge not, and you shall not be judged. Condemn not, and you shall not be condemned. Forgive and you will be forgiven.

Give, and it will be given to you: good measure, pressed down, shaken together, and running over will be put into your bosom.

For with the same measure that you use, it will be measured back to you.

—LUKE 6:37-38

Have you considered why the good measure multiplication Scripture is after the forgiveness Scripture? I believe this juxtaposition is evidence that our restoration, is based on obedience to God's commandments. Wrong attitudes and actions that are contrary to the Word of God thwart, limit and stop the flow of God's blessings to us.

I recall being asked to speak at a prison ministry banquet to raise funds for the ministry. Several days before the event, I sought the LORD on what to speak. As I prayed, the LORD showed a vision of the event, and I saw myself speaking on Luke 6:37-38. The LORD then said (paraphrased),

> "I am assigning restoration angels to this event. Whoever gives to the prison ministry this night will have restoration angels assigned to their lives to bring about their own restoration."

The LORD also showed He would be weighing the hearts of the people based on Luke 6:36-37. Individuals who had a heart of mercy and pardon, not a heart of condemnation or judgment toward those who were incarcerated, would be the individuals who gave an offering. The individuals who gave an offering would be fulfilling Luke 6:37. and in turn, the LORD would respond by fulfilling Luke 6:38. I don't know how many people responded in giving that evening, but I have never forgotten the Counsel of the Lord.

The LORD is after our hearts. He is looking for hearts that will beat like His, give like His and pardon like His. The DNA of God's blood fully pardons. A full pardon is the message of the gospel of grace. God is waiting on each one of us to carry out His message and both receive a pardon and issue a pardon to others, for therein lies *our* restoration.

Psalm 66:18 says:

If I regard iniquity in my heart, the Lord will not hear me.

Iniquity in our heart closes the ears of God to our cries and stops His hand of help and deliverance. Not fully pardoning is iniquity.

Consider this prayer:

PRAYER

Father, I ask You to reveal each person I have not pardoned. I ask You to help me receive from You a pardon for all past sin. I receive the power of Your blood to cleanse my conscience, and to remove the memory of past sin. I receive the power of Your blood to cleanse my conscience.

I repent of not receiving a pardon for my own sins and for continuing to remind You and others of the sins I have committed in my past. I repent for not extending a pardon to others for things they have done or said, and I repent for reminding others of their past sins. I ask You to forgive me and cleanse me of this iniquity.

I receive into my heart and soul a pardon from You and I extend that pardon to others. Thank You that You have promised that if I confess my sins, You are faithful and just to forgive me of all sin and to cleanse me from all unrighteousness.

AMEN

I have good news for you, whoever you are and wherever you are in your walk of faith, the Scripture declares,

According to your faith, be it unto you.

—MATTHEW 9:17

It takes faith to issue and receive a pardon, and it takes faith to obey God's Word. Restoration requires faith. Receiving a pardon and issuing a pardon to others is faith.

Two blind men followed Jesus crying out and saying, "Son of David, have mercy on us!"

Jesus went into a home, and the two blind men followed him. Jesus said to them, "Do you believe that I am able to do this?"

And the men said, "Yes, Lord."

Jesus touched their eyes, saying, "According to your faith, let it be to you."

The Greek word for "believe" used here in Matthew 9 is the word *pisteuo,* which means to be persuaded firmly as to something with the idea of hope and certain expectation. It is the same word used in Romans 4:18 when describing that Abraham *believed* God against all hope, and this belief that was accounted to Abraham as righteousness. In this account, Jesus asked the blind men, "Do you have the faith of Abraham?" In other words, the measure of the blind men's faith determined what God was able to do in their lives.

Cultivating a heart of obedience and faith takes time and effort. An Isaiah 58 fast is a key for cultivating a heart of obedience and a heart of faith, a heart that wholly follows the Lord.

The only instruction found in the Word of God given by Mary, the earthly mother of Jesus Christ, is found John 2 when Mary declares to servants at a wedding feast, "Whatever He says to you, do it." This comment was made during a wedding when the host of the wedding had run out of wine. Mary looked to her Son to assist in supplying more wine. In response, Jesus instructed the servants to "fill the water pots with water" and after doing so to "draw some water out now and take it to the master of the feast." When the master of the feast tasted the water made to wine he proclaimed, "Every man at the beginning sets out the good wine, and when the guests have well drunk, then the inferior. You have kept the good wine until now!"

When the servants followed the instruction of Jesus, the needed miracle occurred: the LORD turned the water into wine and gave an overflow of supply. The master of the house spoke rightly when he said that the "good wine" had been kept until now. That "good wine" is the best wine in the House of God, and it has been kept for you and for me. It is the "good wine" found in the person and power of the third person of the Trinity, the Holy Spirit. It is this "good wine," the Holy Spirit living in and activated in our lives, that makes following the LORD and being fully and firmly persuaded of His promises possible.

Decide today that you are going to follow the LORD through surrendering to the person and power of the Holy Spirit. Decide today to heed the instruction Mary gave to the servants of Jesus, "Anything He says to you, do it." Choose today to pursue diligently and cultivate actively a heart of obedience and expectant, fully convinced faith. Maybe your heart has become hardened and you have little faith left in your heart. An Isaiah 58 fast is God's remedy to break up the fallow ground of a hardened heart so you can once again cry out to the LORD and relentlessly follow Him like the two blind men in order to receive your restoration.

During a fast, the Holy Spirit instructed me to give a specific offering in mercy. After I released the offering the LORD said, "This offering is to remove hardness from your heart." I was somewhat surprised, but then considered the statement. We all have areas in our hearts that have become hardened. It might be a small area or large area, but no matter what the size, we need the LORD to remove hardness from our hearts in order to obediently and sincerely follow the LORD.

Jesus said that if we believe Him as the Scripture has said, then out of our hearts will flow rivers of living water. If we have a hardened, stony or uncultivated heart, the Spirit of God is unable to flow rivers of living water.

Whatever the LORD says to you "do it." Decide today to follow the LORD. This decision will never be regretted on Earth or in heaven and is a sure and certain path to *Divine Restoration.*

$\mathcal{C}$LOSING

$\mathcal{T}$his book began by declaring the Counsel of the LORD for restoration as proclaimed through the prophets Isaiah and Jeremiah as well as through the Apostle Peter. It is on the foundation of the Apostles and Prophets that the Lord Jesus Christ builds His church.[210] Both Isaiah's and Jeremiah's letters declared the Word of the LORD to the exiles living in the Babylonian Dispersion. The letters brought hope and comfort by exhorting the exiles to return to the LORD with all their hearts, to hear *and* to obey the law of the LORD and return to pursing justice, righteousness, truth and equity in their doings with each other. The LORD promised to bring His presence into their lives, which would result in the restoration of their lives and their land.

The Apostle Peter declared that times of refreshing would come from the *presence of the Lord* to those who repent and receive the "blotting out

---

210. Ephesians 2:20

of sin."[211] Later Peter wrote a letter of exhortation to the "pilgrims of the Dispersion," Christians living in various parts of Asia Minor who were suffering rejection in the world because of their obedience to Christ. Peter begins the epistle by reminding the dispersed Christians that their inheritance in Jesus Christ is a hope that is imperishable, undefiled and does not fade away.[212] This inheritance is reserved in heaven for every believer in Jesus Christ. The Greek word for "imperishable" is the word *aphthartos* and means indissoluble, permanent, endless. The Greek word for "undefiled" is the word *amiantos* and means unpolluted, unstained by sin, pure, free from evil.

Our inheritance in heaven is permanent and endless. It consists of living forever as a citizen of a Kingdom, a Kingdom with a ruling King who rules in perfect peace, justice and righteousness.

Isaiah foretells of the glories of this Kingdom:

For a child will be born to us, a Son, will be given to us; and the government will rest on His shoulders; and His name will be called Wonderful, Counselor, Mighty God, Eternal Father, Prince of Peace.

There will be no end to the increase of His government or of peace, On the Throne of David and over His kingdom to establish it and to uphold it with justice and righteousness from then on and forevermore. The zeal of the LORD of hosts will accomplish this.

—ISAIAH 9:6-7, NASB

---

211. Acts 3:19

212. 1 Peter 1:4

The LORD's eternal Kingdom will be a government which governs and rules in peace and one that is established with justice and righteousness. Although Isaiah described the glories of the future Kingdom of God, this future Kingdom is also meant to become a present reality in our lives through the rule of Jesus Christ in our hearts. Divine Restoration is manifested in our lives when the King of Kings, the LORD Jesus Christ rules and reigns in our hearts. The Apostle Paul states that which was once a mystery, has now been revealed: Christ in you, the hope of glory.[213]

Psalm 8:4-9 states that God has crowned man with glory and honor and made him to have dominion over all the works of His hands:

> What is man that You are mindful of him, and the son of man that You visit him?
>
> For You have made him a little lower than the angels, and You have crowned him with *glory* and *honor*.
>
> You have made him to have *dominion* over the works of Your hands; You have put all things under his feet,
>
> All sheep and oxen—even the beasts of the field, the birds of the air, and the fish of the sea that pass through the paths of the seas.
>
> O LORD, our Lord, how excellent is Your name in all the earth!

The Hebrew word for "glory" used in this Psalm is the word *chabod* and means weightiness, heavy, glory, honor, splendor. *Chabod* is God's glory, not only His honor, renown and majesty, but also His visible splendor. The Hebrew word for "honor" is the word *hadar* and also

---

213. Colossians 1:27

means splendor, glory, adornment, magnificence and comes from the verb *hadar* which means "to honor, to glorify and to make splendid." *Hadar* speaks to the honor that is God's and the honor God has bestowed on man. Psalm 8 tell us a most amazing fact: God has crowned man with the glory and splendor, magnificence and honor that belong to God.

Psalm 8:6 reaffirms God's plan for man to have dominion on Earth. The Hebrew word used for "dominion' in Psalm 8 is the word *marshal* and means to govern, have power and reign. God created man to govern and reign over the affairs of Earth in order to establish His peace, justice and righteousness.[214] This responsibility makes man accountable for the conditions and happenings on Earth.

Isaiah 59 outlines the results attributed to man for his failure to obey the mandate and Counsel of God. Yet, Isaiah 58 outlines a key offered from God, to reverse man's failure. Through an Isaiah 58 fast:

- yokes of sin and oppression weaved over our lives are broken;

- barriers to peace, justice and righteousness between man to his fellow man are removed;

- hindrances to God's Counsel of truth are eliminated so that the Spirit of the Lord can enter into our lives;

- having entered, the Spirit of the Lord is then unhindered in bringing the restoration of all things and times of refreshing.

When the conditions outlined in Isaiah 59 are removed, peace can rule men's hearts and righteousness, justice, truth and equity can enter Earth to restore all things back to the original design of the Father.

---

214. Genesis 1:28, Isaiah 9:7, Matthew 28:16-30, Col.1:24-29

When webs of lies are removed, we begin to experience the presence of God in every aspect of our lives. The physical earth begins to respond to God's Spirit.[215] Earth begins to bear fruit, and the ground begins to produce an increase because the dew of heaven can enter and fertile the ground.[216]

When webs are removed, you and all those around you experience salvation (*soteria*—deliverance, soundness, prosperity, happiness, rescue and well-being) on Earth as it is in heaven. When webs of lies are removed, the living Word of God becomes alive and activated within you to transform you and the circumstances around you. When webs of lies are removed, creation *around* you begins to respond to the living Word of God *in* you. Acceleration, multiplication and increase in the fruit of your labors are the result.

CLOUDS

When I was "caught up" and met the LORD in the clouds, and webs were displayed over the face of Earth, I studied the meaning of clouds in the Scripture. Clouds represent the LORD's guiding presence, instruction, protection and glory. The LORD led the children of Israel out of slavery in Egypt through a wilderness land, a place Israel had never walked, by a pillar of cloud by day.[217] During the wilderness journey, the LORD visited Moses in a thick cloud that covered the top of Mt. Sinai, "so the people may hear the LORD and believe Moses forever."[218] Then the LORD called Moses up to the top of Mt. Sinai to meet with Him in the cloud to give him tablets of stone, the Law and

---

215. Zechariah 8:12, Malachi 3:11, Hosea 21:23

216. Zechariah 8:12

217. Exodus 13:21

218. Exodus 19:9

commandments. When Moses went up the mountain, a cloud covered the mountain and the glory of the LORD rested on Mt. Sinai for six days. On the seventh day, the LORD called to Moses out of the midst of the cloud, and Moses went up the mountain into the midst of the cloud and was there forty days and forty nights.[219]

For the first time in the history of the world, God appeared to and spoke to a nation from a cloud. When Jesus Christ the Messiah returns to Earth, the Scriptures declare that He will likewise return in the clouds, and we who are alive will be *caught up* to meet Him:

> For the Lord Himself will descend from heaven with a shout, with the voice of an archangel, and with the trumpet of God. And the dead in Christ will rise first. Then we who are alive and remain shall be *caught up* together with them in the clouds to meet the Lord in the air. And thus we shall always be with the Lord.
>
> —1 THESSALONIANS 4:16-17

The message God gave to Isaiah in chapters 58 and 59 is a message of counsel, instruction, protection and glory—it is a message of hope. It is a message given to cause us to evaluate our hearts and actions. It is a message given to prepare our hearts and lives before the LORD returns. It is a message of Divine Counsel to understand that which has caused estrangement from God and to instruct us in how to return to the LORD.

If a web of lies and iniquity continues, the end of those covered in lies is separation from God. The Apostle Peter reminds us that God is not slack concerning the promise of His return, but is longsuffering

---

219. Exodus 24:12-18

toward us, not willing that any should perish but that all should come to repentance.[220]

GOD IS READY

There is an undeniable truth concerning restoration: separation from God is the problem, and union with God is the answer.

During a trip to New York City, I visited the Eldridge Street Synagogue. This is the oldest synagogue in the United States, built in 1887 by Eastern European immigrants who came to the shores of the United States seeking refuge and freedom. By the 1950s the Synagogue was unable to pay its operating costs. The congregation closed the main sanctuary and moved downstairs to the *bes medrash* to worship.

By the early 1970s, the main sanctuary had water leaks, rotted wood, crumbled plaster and windows had broken due to deterioration. In 1971, a New York University professor brought attention and recognition to the Synagogue that lead to a 25-year restoration project that began in 1986. In 1996, the Synagogue was designated a National Historic Landmark, and in October 2010, the restoration was completed.

I toured the beautifully restored Synagogue and was taken to the east side of the building where the replica of the Ark stood. The guide and I walked up to the platform and opened the Ark. Located therein was a three-tiered platform that accommodated as many as 24 Torah scrolls. As the guide opened the Ark, I was shown the miraculously preserved 1887 crimson red velvet lining where Torah scrolls were housed, the only place in the Synagogue completely preserved for the last 120 plus years. As I touched the original velvet lining, I considered how God had distinctly preserved the compartment where His holy and inspired

---

220. 2 Peter 3:9

Word was housed. In doing so, I was reminded of the eternal words spoken by the prophet Isaiah:

> "The grass withers, the flower fades, but the Word of our God stands forever."

> —ISAIAH 40:8

As you pursue the Counsel of the LORD consider this certainty: you are agreeing with the eternal, unchangeable, immutable and all-powerful living Word of Almighty God. If I could counsel you to do anything it would be to believe, receive, obey and apply actively by faith the living and eternal Word of God. It is the only way to *Divine Restoration*. It is the Counsel of the LORD.

> He sent His word and healed them, and delivered them from their destructions.

> Oh, that men would give thanks to the LORD for His goodness, and for His wonderful works to the children of men!

> —PSALM 107:20-21

ARE YOU CERTAIN?

DO YOU KNOW FOR SURE
THAT YOU HAVE ETERNAL LIFE?

If you were to die today, do you know for certain that you would go to heaven? Do you have an eternal relationship with God? Suppose you were to die tonight and stand before God, and He was to say to you, "Why should I let you into heaven," what would you say?

If you don't know how you would answer those two questions, I have good news for you. The Bible tells us emphatically that it was written so you might know for certain how you can have an eternal relationship with God the Father.

The Bible was inspired by the Holy Spirit of God operating through His prophets and apostles. From Genesis to Revelation, all Scripture points us to an eternal relationship with God the Father, offered through the atonement of Jesus Christ the Messiah, Yeshua Ha-Mashiach.

The Bible says that an eternal relationship with God is offered to man as a gift, we cannot earn it or deserve it.

> For by God's grace we have been saved through faith, and that not of ourselves, it is the gift of God, not of works lest anyone should boast.
>
> —EPHESIANS 2:8-9

> For the wages of sin is death, but the gift of God is eternal life through Jesus Christ our LORD.
>
> —ROMANS 6:23

The Bible also tells us that man has violated God's law and, therefore, has sinned. The penalty for sin is eternal death and separation from God.

> "…For all have sinned and fall short of the glory of God."
>
> —ROMANS 3:23

> "There is none righteous, no not one."
>
> —ROMANS 3:10

Because God is holy and just, He must punish sin. Exodus 34:7 states that God will by no means clear the guilty. Yet God is love. God loves all men and does not want to punish sin.

> God is love.
>
> —1 JOHN 4:8

> Say to them, "As I live," says the LORD God, "I have no pleasure in the death of the wicked, but that the wicked turn from his way and live."
>
> —EZEKIEL 33:11

Therefore, God the Father had a dilemma: God loves man, but He must punish man's sin because He is holy and just. God solved this dilemma in the Person of Jesus Christ. God the Father sent God the Son, Jesus Christ to Earth, born of a Virgin, conceived by the Holy Spirit, crucified on a Roman cross, raised to life three days later and who has ascended into heaven where He sits at the right hand of God, awaiting His sure and certain return. The Bible says,

> For God so loved the world that He gave His only begotten Son that whoever believes in Him shall not perish but have everlasting life.
>
> —JOHN 3:16

The prophet Isaiah foretold of the Savior's birth and suffering unto death to bear the sins of the world:

> For unto us a Child is born, Unto us a Son is given; and the government will be upon His shoulder. And His name will be called Wonderful, Counselor, Mighty God, Everlasting Father, Prince of Peace. Of the increase of His government and peace there will be no end, upon the throne of David and over His kingdom, to order it and establish it with judgment and justice from that time forward, even forever.
>
> —ISAIAH 9:6-7

Surely He has borne our griefs and carried our sorrows; yet we esteemed Him stricken, smitten by God, and afflicted. But He was wounded for our transgressions, He was bruised for our iniquities; the chastisement for our peace was upon Him, and by His stripes we are healed. All we like sheep have gone astray; we have turned, everyone, to his own way; and the LORD has laid on Him the iniquity of us all.

—ISAIAH 53:4-6

The prophet Isaiah stated the Messiah would come as a Suffering Servant and would bear our griefs, carry our sorrows, be wounded for our transgressions, bruised for our iniquities and by His stripes we are healed. Isaiah 53 describes the substitutionary death of the Messiah. The substitutionary death must happen because the Scripture tells us that there can be no remission (sending away, release from bondage, forgiveness) for sin without the shedding of blood (Leviticus 17:11, Hebrews 9:22). Perfect blood—divine blood—holy blood, is the only blood that can cleanse the heart and conscience of man from the curse and effect of sin (Hebrews 9:11-15).

For this reason, God sent the perfect likeness of Himself to Earth to become the Suffering Servant. God the Father sent the Person of Jesus Christ, Yeshuah the Messiah. The Scripture says in John 10:30 that, "I (Jesus Christ) and my Father are one."

This is the Gospel of the Kingdom of God. This is the good news— that God came to Earth to die for you and me and was raised to life on the third day so you and I could receive reconciliation back to the Father. Reconciliation is offered as a gift of God's grace and is received by faith.

Faith is the key that opens the door to heaven. Faith is not simply having a head knowledge of facts about Jesus Christ. Faith is not simply believing God for temporary things, like praying for help to get you through a sickness or seeking help with a job or finances, your children or family. This is temporary faith. Once the problem or need is over, your faith is over.

Faith is also not trusting in your own "goodness" or good deeds to get you into heaven by thinking, "I have been a pretty good person, so I think God will let me into heaven," or thinking, "God is merciful, and I think He would let me into heaven." Faith is also not trusting in some type of penance, corporate or family religion or fulfilling some type of religious "rites." These outward forms of godliness alone, will never bring you into an eternal relationship with God the Father, no matter how devoted, loyal and sincere you are in doing them.

Eternal life is only possible through a spiritual birth that comes from a change of heart. A change of the heart is only possible after sincere repentance—having a change of mind about personal sin and rebellion to God.

However, if you sincerely repent of your sin and rebellion to God and confess with your mouth the Lord Jesus Christ and believe in your heart that God raised Him from the dead you will be saved, for with the heart one believes unto righteousness, and with the mouth confession is made unto salvation (Romans 10:9-10). This supernatural experience is called a "new birth" (John 3:3-5).

If you have felt the Holy Spirit knocking on the door of your heart, trust that knock as God's personal invitation to you to have all the sin you have ever committed forgiven. The knock on your heart is God's invitation to you to receive reconciliation back to Him and to receive eternal life. If you have not answered the knock at the door of your heart, or if you have once answered the knock and then later shut the door, it is time to open the door to your heart.

If you have never trusted in Jesus Christ as your Lord and Savior and have never surrendered your heart and life to God, or if you have turned away from God and need to return to Him, below is a prayer you can offer to the LORD.

Dear Father,

I have heard Your good news. I understand that eternal life with you is a gift. Today is my day to receive Your gift to me. I ask You to forgive me of my sins and my rebellion to You. I acknowledge that I am separated from You because of my sin.

I choose today to repent and turn away from sin and rebellion toward You. I come to You with all my heart and mind. I acknowledge that You are Holy and that You cannot look upon my sin. Today I receive what Your Son, Your Only Son—Jesus Christ did for me when He died on a Roman cross. Today I receive payment for my sins offered to me through the death of Jesus Christ, and I receive restoration back to You.

By faith, I come, and I ask You, Jesus Christ, to come into my heart and be my Savior and my Lord. I open my heart to You, Jesus Christ. I ask You to come into my heart and bring Your cleansing blood, peace and light. I ask You to fill me up with the power of Your Holy Spirit.

Thank You, Jesus, for forgiving me and for coming into my heart as my Savior and my Lord. Thank you, Jesus, for bringing salvation to me today and for writing my name in your book of Life.

ABOUT THE AUTHOR

CHRISTINA L. MCCRACKEN, J.D.

Christina L. McCracken is a lawyer, counselor and friend of God. The daughter of a trial lawyer, Christina grew up advocating for fairness and justice. She wanted to be a missionary and beckoned God for this calling, only to hear the words, "No, you are going to practice law." Over time, God revealed the intentions of His calling for her life— to become an advocate for God by contending for the removal of "webs of lies" off individuals, cities and nations and for the manifestation of God's justice, righteousness, equity and truth to be revealed in the lives of God's people.

Drawing from her intimate relationship with Jesus Christ, 28 years as a lawyer and advocate and decades as a bible-teacher and minister of the Word of God, she brings practical counsel and wisdom in her advocacy for restoration. She is the author of *Live for That Day: Overcome Your Mountain, Garnering Rewards at the Judgment Seat of Christ* and is married to the love of her life.